COMPREHENSIVE
CHESS
COURSE

VOLUME I *Learn Chess in 12 lessons*

W9-DEE-855

BY ROMAN PELTS
AND GM LEV ALBURT,
three-time U.S. Chess Champion

THE COMPLETE, EASY-TO-USE PROGRAM FOR TEACHING AND SELF-STUDY

Volume I

The Rules of Play:
12 Lessons For The Beginning Chessplayer

Level One
of
The Comprehensive Program of Chess Training

by Roman Pelts
and GM Lev Alburt, three-time U.S. Champion

Copyright 1986, 1987, 1992, 1996 by Roman Pelts and Lev Alburt
4th, revised edition

Chess Information and Research Center
P.O. Box 534, Gracie Station, New York, NY 10028
For ordering information, see last page.

Library of Congress card number: 96-85865
ISBN 1-889323-00-4
Distribution to book trade in North America:
W.W. Norton, 500 Fifth Avenue, New York City.

Photographer: Nigel Eddis
Cover: Anna Malova, former Miss Russia, explains knight moves to Tatiana Eddis.

Printed in the United States of America.

TABLE OF CONTENTS

VOLUME I: AN INTRODUCTION

*C*omprehensive Chess Course is primarily intended to serve as a manual for those teaching chess in schools and colleges and for parents teaching chess to their children or, for that matter, to themselves. From California to New York, this course has been employed successfully in numerous scholastic programs. Since 1986 and through two editions (plus several printings), thousands of players have purchased this course for self-study. And if letters from our readers are any guide, then thousands have used this course to enter fully the world of chess or to progress from beginner status to advanced levels.

The success of *Comprehensive Chess Course* has been gratifying to both of the authors, though we must admit not too surprising. At the risk of appearing immodest, we were confident that the course would be well-received because of its unique origins and proven record of success in the former Soviet Union.

Soviet chess education owed a lot to the famous Moscow 1925 international, during which Russian scientists tested several of the competitors and published a landmark study, *The Psychology of Chess Play*. By the late 1920s, chess was being taught to hundreds of thousands of students in the expectation that it would provide them with valuable intellectual training. The instructors of that period — as they do today — conducted chess classes according to an approved program. At the end of each school year, the teachers out in the field would meet in seminars with national-level chess officials to discuss curricular weaknesses.

By the early 1960s an unusually effective program had been honed through the trial and error of decades-long experience. Over a period of four to five years, attentive students could expect to reach the 2200-level with a weekly input of a single two-hour lesson, buttressed by four hours of homework and another two to three hours of practical play. This total of eight to nine hours a week compares favorably with the amount of time that many American players spend pushing wood in their clubs and homes.

Numerous Soviet grandmasters were raised on this course, including Lev Alburt, one of the authors of this volume. Alburt's coach in the former Soviet Union was FM Roman Pelts. When Pelts left the U.S.S.R. several years ago, he smuggled out the course (never published in book form) in small notebooks that he listed as his personal notes.

Comprehensive Chess Course, Volume I

(level 1) that the reader holds in his hand, is an updated and improved version of the first portion of the multi-year Soviet course. This portion is designed to bring the reader to approximately Class C strength. Its pedagogical method is to provide the reader *only* with the knowledge required — no more and no less — to progress from level to level. No other books are necessary to reach the given goals if the material becomes part of the student's *active* knowledge, which is to say, knowledge that can be readily applied in practical play.

Readers who have completed Volumes I and II of *Comprehensive Chess Course* frequently ask what to do next. How can they consolidate what they have learned, and how can they increase their strength further? In this third revised edition, we have included at the end of Volume II a chapter titled, "Moving On to Expert and Master." In this chapter we recommend a study and training regimen that was used by Grandmaster Alburt himself. In addition, we recommend several books on tactics, the endgame and the opening to aid in the advance to expert and master.

Several readers want to know when we intend to publish a third volume in our *Comprehensive Chess Course*. The greatest difficulty is the sheer size of such a volume. It is no accident that Volume I is less than half the length of Volume II. The amount of knowledge required to progress from one level to another increases geometrically. We estimate that the next portion of our course requires about 1,000 pages to provide the knowledge necessary to reach expert strength. Instead of producing one huge volume we've decided to divide this bulk of material into six or seven books. The first level III book, *Chess Tactics for the Tournament Player* was published in November 1995.

Books on attack and defense, strategy, endings, and openings will soon follow.

GETTING STARTED
No prior knowledge of chess is presupposed in *Comprehensive Chess Course*. Experience suggests that children will require about three months to complete the beginners' course of 12 lessons, while adults will need roughly two months. After completing the first five lessons

during the first month of study, the student will be acquainted with the moves of all the pieces and will know what is meant by checkmating the opponent.

Chess classes should preferably have no more than a dozen students, and lessons ought to be held once a week. A lesson normally lasts 90 minutes, but since it is difficult for children under age 10 to concentrate for so long, lessons for them should not exceed one hour. By the same token, lessons for adults may be extended to two hours. Our experience indicates that whatever the total time of a lesson, it should be split evenly between the theoretical segment (steps 1 to 4 below) and the practical (step five below). Here is our recommended lesson plan:

1. Check homework, if necessary.
2. Review previously studied material.
   (Steps 1 and 2 taken together ought not to exceed 10 to 15 minutes.)
3. Introduce new material.
4. Assign homework for the next lesson.
   (Steps 3 and 4 taken together ought to consume 30 to 35 minutes.)
5. Play practice games for about 45 minutes.

GETTING TO KNOW CHESS
Chess, one of the oldest games extant, has been fascinating and challenging people for some 1,500 years. This game of thought, fantasy and planning remains, in spite of its hoary origins, eminently suited to the needs of modern man. Indeed, if chess was once called the "royal game," it is today a pastime for everyman — a pursuit that combines relaxation with intellectual exercise. It is one of the few things in life that is fun, free, non-fattening and moral.

The benefits that children derive from chess can hardly be overestimated. Children who start learning chess show great improvement in mathematics, in physics and in the capability to do independent research. Studies have shown that regular chess training develops a child's powers of concentration and the facility for thinking logically. The competitive aspect — especially the struggle to save lost positions — also builds willpower. "Never give up" is a sound idea in both chess and life.

Many people want to learn chess but do not know how to go about it in the correct way. Some try to learn on their own but often fail. Teaching chess to others is still more difficult. Even professional players may lack the skills to teach chess. Many of these chess paladins land up sending their children to experienced chess coaches.

Most parents, however, do not have such an alternative and try to teach their children with the help of books. Nowadays, many chess books for children are available, but some of them simply ignore modern methods of instruction. They were either written long ago or, so to speak, ought to have been.

In *Comprehensive Chess Course*, we have divided into several levels the climb upwards from beginner. To progress from one level to the next, a student must acquire a certain amount of theoretical knowledge and practical strength. The precise amount of knowledge that he must master is determined by his level. If a student acquires too much knowledge for his particular level, he will not benefit from it and could even be harmed by it. Too many students expend time and energy learning what they do not yet need to know and become discouraged when practical results do not correspond to effort.

The basic principle of *Comprehensive Chess Course* is that at each level a student should study chess in a manner appropriate to that level. Openings, for example, are studied at all course levels but in a steadily more thorough and profound fashion.

The lessons and methodological instructions provided in this book are self-contained, so that coaches can guide their students through the entire program without additional literature. Yet coaches are allowed plenty of room to teach creatively. Depending on the age of students, coaches may increase or decrease lesson material so long as fundamental methodological principles are not contravened. For instance, coaches may decide to use only a few of the many problems provided in each lesson if the students appear to be mastering the material easily.

A good chess coach has two aims:

1. To teach children to play chess correctly, which requires that they think logically and self-critically; and
2. To instill in children an appreciation for the beauty of chess ideas so that they will enjoy playing the game.

One can hardly overemphasize the importance of kindling genuine interest in chess during the very first lessons. Children usually find their initial chess lesson to be the most difficult, which is where parents can help out by explaining the rules at home.

By our joint efforts, we can initiate children — in fact, your children — into the wonders of chess. They will thereby have the opportunity of spending many happy hours in the future exploring the mysteries of mankind's greatest game.

COMPREHENSIVE SELF–STUDY

Before discussing in detail the teaching of chess in classroom situations, we note that not every student can have a coach, and many adults who wish to learn chess lack the time to attend classes. For these individuals, *Comprehensive Chess Course* can serve as an ideal self-study guide. Virtually all material is self-explanatory, and students can utilize volumes I and II profitably.

Two quick tips: 1. When asked to solve problems or to answer various questions, we recommend that players spend no more than five to 10 minutes on most positions; the point is not so much to test yourself as to *understand* the chess meaning of the answers given elsewhere and to acquire needed knowledge; and 2. One difficulty in self-study is to discover when one's knowledge moves from being theoretical in nature to being active, which is to say, knowledge that can be easily applied in practice. We recommend that self-study students — both children and adults — take all of the examinations provided in Volume I and, when possible, play practice games at chess clubs or elsewhere.

Finally, although sections of Volume I are elementary for players well-acquainted with the rules, this volume nonetheless contains much that ought to be in every player's arsenal and often is not. For example, how complete is *your* knowledge of the chessboard? Quick, what color is the d6 square? What color is f7? There should be no hesitation in your answers. Okay, here is what ought to be an easy one: White has pawns on a6 and b6 and a King on e2; Black has a Rook on c5 and a King on g5. With the second player to move, can he stop the pawns? Yes or no, quickly!

Well, you get the idea. Use Volume I to master basic knowledge that you should be able to employ effortlessly.

TEACHING CHESS

The methods and goals of teaching chess are similar to those when teaching any other subject. We want to educate students, develop their native abilities and impart habits useful for further advancement. To teach chess productively, one proceeds from the simple to the complex, all the while maintaining an unity between theory and practice and a sound relationship between instructors and pupils.

Comprehensive Chess Course is based on the method of repeatedly presenting certain problems to students, though in modified forms. The idea is that the problems, while retaining their previous characteristics, are made more complicated by the addition of new ideas. Take, for example, the idea of double attack. It can be found in the games of both tyros and world titleholders and is obviously a device that can be used by chess players of all strengths. When teaching this idea to a Class D player, the following position might be used:

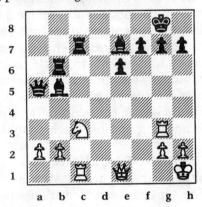

The correct move for White is **1. Qe5**, which attacks the Rook on c7 and threatens mate on g7.

At a more advanced level, the above position can be altered to show how the concept of double attack can serve as the basis for multi-move combinations.

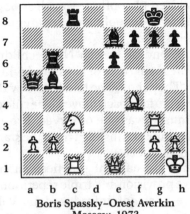

Boris Spassky–Orest Averkin
Moscow, 1973

White wins by creating a double attack after **1. Bc7! Rxc7 2. Qe5** (once again, White attacks the Rook on c7 and threatens mate on g7) **2. ... g6 3. Qxc7.**

Utilizing a progression of difficulty as illustrated in the above two diagrams, new themes are introduced on the basis of previously studied material, thereby broadening the student's knowledge and helping him to assimilate efficiently previously mastered subject matter.

Teachers must explain and demonstrate to their pupils every new item before assigning the relevant homework. The division of material between homework and work done in class is completely up to the coach. A key point to remember is that children are primarily attracted to chess as a game and that plenty of time should be allocated to playing the game. Yes, the rules of the game are very important, but children love to compete against one another. Do not skimp on the practical element.

Coaches should be completely sure that students have mastered the subject matter before moving on to the next lesson. Not a single lesson should be skipped. Progress can only be made when students thoroughly study the material. And, of course, do not lose sight of the obvious: Only when students have understood a given item can they properly apply it in their games.

Chess lessons can last until the children show signs of weariness. Quality of learning is more important than quantity. When the students compete against one another, they should not be encouraged to play quick games. Instead, they should consider every move carefully. Let the children play often — against opponents ranging from schoolmates to parents to computers.

By the end of Lesson Nine, children will know the main rules of chess and will be able to play. They should be told to follow the rules and never to take back moves. The rule of touch move must always be observed. Proper playing habits must be instilled from the start if they are to take effect.

Formal tournament practices such as the 50-move provision and triple repetition of position are best not introduced in Volume I, which is meant to get a beginner *playing* chess as soon as possible and to provide him with the necessary knowledge to proceed to Volume II.

One pitfall to avoid is simplifying the subject matter too much in a desire to assure that it is understood by students. With all challenge removed from the learning process, many children lose interest. There are weak, average and strong players in every group, and best results are usually obtained by planning lessons for above-average students, while motivating slower students to become over-achievers. In a group of 10 students, veteran coaches typically peg the lessons to the third strongest player and enlist the top two players to assist them in teaching.

If any students have questions that were not cleared up in the theoretical half of the lesson, then the coach can work with these students during the practical portion of the lesson. The key here is to adopt an individual approach to the students, and if a coach believes that a player is strong enough to study material in Volume II, then he should give the student a battery of tests from Volume I. The tests in Volume I may also be given to newcomers to determine their class or level assignment.

We recommend strongly that in a lesson involving, say, 10 students, there be at least 12 sets available. The pieces should be set up, and during the first half of the lesson — the theoretical segment — each student should have a separate set. It is advisable that the pieces be large, plastic and of simple design. Such sets are easily available and inexpensive. The boards should be large enough for the pieces to seem smaller than the squares. The teacher should have a demonstration board and two additional sets at his command.

VISUALIZATION: THE KEY TO SUCCESS

All beginning chess players should start by studying and memorizing the chessboard. Knowing the board by heart has great importance because of the vital relationship between playing strength and the facility of being able to visualize the chessboard and chessmen.

We provide a whole series of exercises to help students in the task of memorizing the board. Depending on the aptitudes of students, three to 10 hours are typically devoted to learning the board. A student's knowledge of the board should be perfect in the sense that visualizing the board becomes automatic. To ensure that students develop the habit of visualization, coaches ought to set aside a few minutes of every lesson from Volume I for board drills. Knowledge of the chessboard is to aspiring players what mastery of multiplication tables is to children studying arithmetic. It borders on the essential.

As lesson follows lesson, the chessboard will contain more and more pawns and pieces, and students who have a sound knowledge of the 64 squares will acquire the knack of visualizing mentally those positions that could occur on the board a few moves ahead.

As mentioned earlier, coaches must demonstrate on a chessboard all problems and examples to students in the first stages of instruction. Not only are such demonstrations necessary for students to tackle their homework, but they also aid players in memorizing the board. Never forget that for beginners, a chessboard is what educators call a "visual aid" and is an indispensable teaching tool.

NOTES ABOUT VOLUME I

In Volume I, the beginner learns the simplest relationships between the various chessmen. As far as the opening is concerned, the material in Volume I provides students with the main principles governing the mobilization of forces, which include rapid development of Knights and Bishops, the importance of controlling the center, the disadvantages of bringing out the Queen too early, the problems with pushing flank pawns, and castling.

Beginners studying Volume I acquire a mastery of the algebraic system of notation, which is the system employed in succeeding levels of our chess program. Later on, students will also be introduced to descriptive notation. Of the two systems, algebraic enjoys certain important advantages over descriptive. It is generally more concise, simplifies the process of learning and is internationally recognized. Experience demonstrates that algebraic causes no difficulties for students, and even eight-year-old children can use it after completing Volume I. Readers will notice that we use chess diagrams with ranks and files marked with the appropriate numbers and letters — a good technique for helping students to master algebraic notation and for aiding memorization of the board. We encourage coaches to use chessboards with such markings.

Systematic checking of a student's knowledge is very important in teaching chess. *Comprehensive Chess Course* contains within it material meant to reinforce earlier lessons, but teachers must also play their part. Do not forget to review earlier material promptly, which is to say, before students have started to forget the subject matter. Our course provides coaches with sufficient questions and tests to perform the vital review function, and they may be employed according to a coach's best judgment. The idea here is to maintain the unity of theory and practice.

When drilling students, coaches ought to ask good students difficult questions and slower students easier ones. Obvious, yes. But the reason for this practice is a bit less obvious. Questions help to activate a student's learning process, and if he can answer questions and solve problems about material that he has studied, then he acquires the vital asset of self-confidence.

Avoid pairing a relatively strong player with a weak one because the latter will soon lose interest when defeats come too fast and too often. Coaches must be sure to assign children to groups at their own level and to find them suitable playing partners. This requirement is particularly important for beginners because at higher levels, when children have already acquired a certain understanding and love of chess, they will treat their losses differently and will not become discouraged so easily. The guiding principle during the first lessons of Volume I is to separate absolute beginners from those who already play a little.

Coaches cannot possibly examine every game played by students during a lesson. They ought to select the most typical errors and explain how to avoid them. They should also point out games in which players have skillfully applied material that they studied. Further, coaches should show students how to record their moves so that they can later conduct post-mortems, which are detailed analytical sessions following games.

Coaches must stress to players that improvement is a function of studying seriously every day. The strongest players work very hard on chess because they know that there are many formidable opponents, who all want to win. The winners are those who labor systematically to perfect their knowledge and to build their practical competitive strength.

TESTING STUDENTS

Lesson 12, the final chapter of Volume I, contains 20 different tests of six questions each. These tests cover the contents of Volume I, and we recommend that students be allowed 60 minutes to take a single test. Coaches are, of course, free to administer more than one test to their students. Indeed, if a student fails to answer correctly more than three questions, he should be allowed to try another test. Coaches make the decision when a student is ready to move on to Volume II.

We recommend that there be an interval of several weeks between the study of Volume I and Volume II. This interval should be spent for practice games, tournament competition, training with coaches, participation in simultaneous exhibitions, and holding problem-solving contests (with book prizes). These latter events usually feature positions posted on demonstration boards with students receiving three points for a correct answer and losing a point for a wrong answer. In such fashion, students are encouraged to think carefully before answering. Such contests normally consist of three to six problems.

HOMEWORK SUGGESTIONS

Ideally, every student should have a copy of *Comprehensive Chess Course*. Time is saved, and the teacher's task becomes easier. But if such is not possible, then the teacher must make copies for his students of the homework assignments. We strongly urge that answers to the questions be included in the handouts. *When doing homework, a student ought to spend no more than five to 10 minutes on a particular question. If he is unable to answer it, he should then consult the answer and try to understand it.*

Teachers need not go over homework at the start of the next class unless a student has a question or unless the teacher feels that one of the problems is particularly instructive. If the latter, then the teacher should ask one of the students who solved the problem correctly to explain the solution on a demonstration board to the entire class.

Do not encourage students to complete their homework in a single sitting. It is better if they distribute the work over a couple of days, since a fresh outlook when studying will enable players to retain material more completely.

The second segment of each lesson, the period devoted to competitive play, serves much the same purpose as homework. Another benefit of practical competition is that it helps to eliminate or minimize one-move blunders. Beginners react quite poorly to their opponent's threats, typically making a move planned beforehand very quickly. They ignore changes in the position created by their opponent's moves. As a result, the games of beginners abound in one-move blunders which drop pawns and pieces — not to mention the frequent sight of the numerically superior side overlooking an elementary checkmate.

FEAR OF LOSING

A serious difficulty is how to teach children not to fear defeat. Some children stop playing precisely because of this fear of losing. Teachers must explain to students that each lost game contains within it the promise of future improvement — *if the mistakes made (the reasons for losing) are found and understood.* Strong chess players always make a point of analyzing closely their lost games because they know that understanding their chess shortcomings will help them play better in the future.

Once a child has a firm grip on the rules and has acquired some practical experience, he should be encouraged to participate in tournaments.

The material in Volume I can be taught by any school teacher or parent, provided that he plays chess better than his pupils and possesses reasonable teaching skills. If a coach infuses a love of chess in his charges, then he will have given them a gift that can last a lifetime. It is the gift of appreciating the beauty of chess and, in the process, of appreciating the beauty of the human intellect.

The authors would like to acknowledge their indebtedness to those who have aided us in the preparation of *Comprehensive Chess Course*. Jonathan Berry and Indian chess enthusiast Mohan translated the two volumes, and Gordon Howe performed admirable labors as proofreader. For help with preparing the second edition, the authors are very grateful to Faneuil Adams, Dewain Barber, Svetozar Jovanovic, Bruce Pandolfini and others who assisted in this work. Nigel Eddis, the world's leading chess photographer, took the cover photograph. For insightful advice on the new chapter, ''Moving On to Expert and Master,'' we thank Dr. Martin Katahn. And, of course, we thank the many readers who wrote in with suggestions and corrections. Finally, we both wish to thank Lyuba Pelts, the wife of FM Pelts, who aided in the translation of Volume I and who unfailingly attended to the endless small, though vital tasks involved in producing a work such as *Comprehensive Chess Course*.

Roman Pelts and Lev Alburt
New York City
August 1, 1996

Lesson One

Starting Position. How Pawns Move and Capture.

Chess is a very ancient game that first appeared in India around the fourth or fifth century A.D. Although there are many legends about the origin of chess, nobody really knows who invented the game.

Chess is an intellectual competition between two players.

It is played on a square board divided into 64 equal squares that are alternately light and dark. Each player always has a light corner square on his right. Remember: "Light on the Right".

1

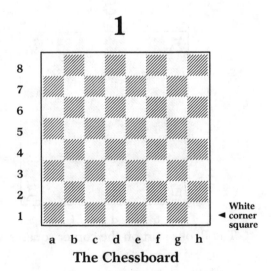

The Chessboard

There are 32 chessmen, 16 White and 16 Black. One of the players has the White men and the other the Black men. Diagram 2 shows how the men are set up at the start of a game. In all chess diagrams the White side is shown as moving up the board and the Black side as moving down the board.

2

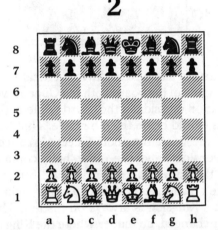

A chessman (or man) means either a pawn or a piece. A pawn is never called a piece. Thus each side at the start of a game has eight pawns and eight pieces. The chart below shows how many of each type of piece each player has, and the symbols usually used to represent the pieces in diagrams.

Name	White	Black	Symbols
King	1	1	K or ♔ ♚
Queen	1	1	Q or ♕ ♛
Rook	2	2	R or ♖ ♜
Bishop	2	2	B or ♗ ♝
Knight	2	2	N or ♘ ♞
pawn	8	8	P or ♙ ♟

Diagram 2 shows the starting position of the men and Diagrams 5–10 show how to set the men up one by one. The player with the White men is called "White," and the player with the Black men is called "Black."

The half of the board on which the White men stand is called the "White Side" and the half with the Black men on it is called the

1

"Black Side." This is shown in Diagram 3, where an imaginary horizontal line separates the White Side from the Black Side.

3

Black's side

White's side

a b c d e f g h

If instead a line were drawn vertically down the middle of the board both the Queens would appear on one side of the board while both the Kings would be on the other side. That half of the board containing both Queens is called the "Queenside" and the other half, containing both the Kings, is known as the "Kingside." White's Kingside is always on his right and Black's Kingside is always on his left. This is never changed, no matter where the Kings and Queens move on the board during the game See Diagram 4.

4

Queen's side   King's side

a b c d e f g h

Each player moves in turn, with White starting. Two consecutive moves by the same player are prohibited by the rules of play. Nor can a player pass his turn. A move is a transfer of a man from the square on which it is, to another

square to which it is permitted by the rules to move.

If an enemy man is on the square to which a move is made, it is captured and removed from the board, and it cannot take part in the game any more. Thus, the number of men in a game of chess can only decrease and never increase. Two men cannot simultaneously occupy the same square, and a player can never capture one of his own men. Each type of chessman has its own way of moving, and all men of the same type move in the same way.

The aim of the game is to capture the opponent's King. The person who succeeds in doing this first is the winner. If neither player succeeds in winning, the game ends in a draw.

Since it is hard to learn the moves of all the different chessmen at one go, we'll take it step by step. Today you will learn the pawn's move and how to play a game using only pawns.

How to Set up Pieces on the Board
Diagrams 5–10

5

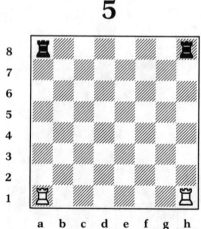

a b c d e f g h

The Rooks start on the corner squares.

6

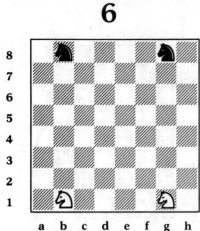

Next to the Rooks go the Knights.

7

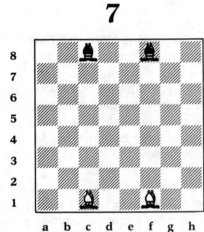

The Bishops go next to the Knights.

8

The Queen always starts on a square of her own color.

9

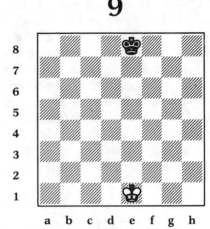

The Kings take the remaining squares — White King on dark square, Black King on light.

10

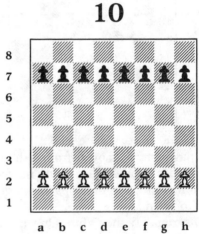

Each side's eight pawns are placed on the row of squares in front of their pieces.

How the Pawn Moves and Captures

Pawns are the smallest of the chessmen. They are valued by experts, but often scorned by beginners. The White pawns start the game on the second rank and move forward, while the Black pawns start the game on the seventh rank and move in the opposite direction, towards the White pawns.

Pawns of the same color all look alike. If we want to identify one of them in particular, we use the name of the piece that it stood in front of in the starting position: the Queen's Rook pawn and the King's Rook pawn, the Queen's

3

Knight pawn and the King's Knight pawn, the Queen's Bishop pawn and the King's Bishop pawn, the Queen's pawn and the King's pawn.

The pawn is the only chessman that cannot move backwards. Nor can it jump over other men. The pawn moves only forward, one square at a time along the file on which it stands. Every pawn, no matter how far the game has progressed, has a choice on its first move (and only on its first move) of moving forward either one or two squares.

12

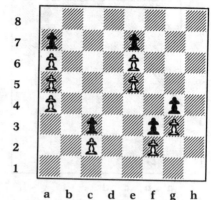

None of the pawns can move.

11

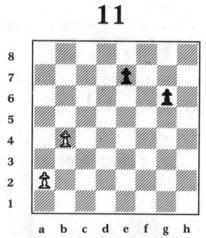

The pawns have moved from White's and Black's sides. The White pawn moved two squares forward, the Black pawn moved one square forward.

In Diagram 11, the White Queen's Knight pawn has moved two squares forward on its first move. This double move is optional. Thus, the Black King's Knight pawn has moved only one square forward on its first move. From now on, these two pawns are allowed to move ahead only one square at a time. On the Queen's Rook file and the King file we can see the move-by-move progress of a pawn from its starting position to the other end of the board.

If a man (either its own or the enemy's) is on the square immediately in front of a pawn, the pawn is blocked and cannot advance. See Diagram 12.

Capturing With the Pawn

The pawn, although it moves straight ahead, captures in a different way. Namely, it captures one square diagonally forward. It cannot capture backwards. Each quarter of Diagram 13 shows an example of a pawn attacking enemy pieces. For example, in 13-I, the White pawn can capture the Black Rook or the Black Knight, but not the Black Bishop. The pawn cannot advance until the Black Bishop gets out of its way. The pawn attacks two squares diagonally ahead of it (one on either side) unless it is a Rook pawn, when it attacks only one square. A capture is carried out in the following way: the pawn moves onto the square occupied by the enemy man, which is removed from the board. Diagrams 13 and 14 show the different ways in which a pawn can capture.

13

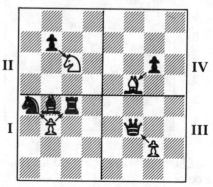

pawn position before capturing

4

14

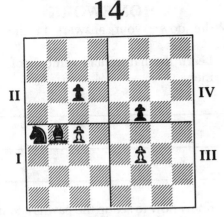

pawn position **after capturing**

15

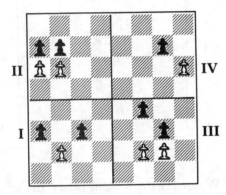

16

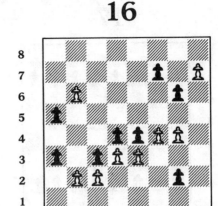

How many different moves can the White and Black pawns make?

Answer: The White pawns can make a total of ten different moves. The Black pawns can also make a total of ten moves.

Now you are ready to play!

I. The White pawn has four possible moves.

II. Each of the four pawns can make a capture, but none of them can advance.

III. Black is threatening to take off White's pawn.

IV. Each pawn can either move forward or capture the opposing pawn.

A pawn which has moved onto a new file by capturing an enemy man advances along this new file even if there is already a pawn of the same color on that file.

In Diagram 12, none of the pawns can move. The middle King pawn could only have got there by capturing. The White King pawns are said to be "doubled." It is quite unusual to have three pawns of the same color on one file, such as the "tripled" pawns on the Rook file in Diagram 12.

Now look at Diagram 16. How many different moves can the White pawns make in all? How many can the Black pawns make in all?

The Pawn Game

Here are the rules:

1. Choosing for colors. One of the players hides a Black pawn in one fist and a White pawn in the other. He then holds out both fists in front of him and the opponent selects one of them. The opponent will play Black if the fist has a Black pawn, and he will play White if it contains a White pawn. After the first game, the players switch colors every game.

2. The Starting Position. The starting position should be as shown in Diagram 17.

5

17

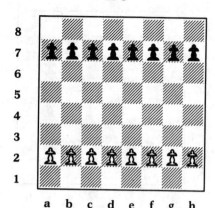

3. You win the game:
a) if your opponent gives up; or
b) if you are the first to capture all your opponent's pawns; or
c) if you are the first to reach the last rank (i.e., your opponent's first rank) with one of your pawns; or
d) if it is your opponent's turn to move but all his pawns are blocked and do not have any moves, while you yourself can make at least one move.

The game is a draw (i.e., a tied game):
a) if the two players agree to call it a draw; or
b) if **both** sides' pawns are blocked up so that **neither** side can make any moves.

Before you start, remember one very important rule: if you touch one of your own men when it is your turn to move, you must move it. If you touch one of your opponent's men, you must capture it if you can. And of course once you make a move, you cannot change it. Get into the habit of playing Touch-Move! First think out your move carefully, and then play it firmly and without hesitation.

HOMEWORK

Write down your answers in the space below.

1. Learn the names and symbols of all the men.

_____

_____

_____

2. Know how to set up the pawns and pieces in the starting position.

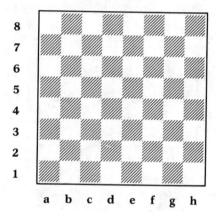

3. Where are the Knights placed in the initial position (between which pieces)?

_____

_____

_____

4. Where are the Bishops placed in the initial position?

_____

_____

_____

5. In the initial position, which men are placed on the corner squares?

_____

_____

_____

6. What color is the right-hand corner square nearest a player?

_____

_____

_____

7. What is the least number of moves in which a pawn starting from its initial position can reach the other end of the board?

_____

_____

_____

8. How many different pawn moves does White have in the starting position?

_____

_____

_____

and a Knight and the other between the King and a Knight (see Diagram 7).

5. The Rooks occupy the corner squares (see Diagram 5).

6. A player's lower right-hand corner square is always a light square. Remember: "light on the right!"

7. A pawn needs five moves from its original square to reach the other end of the board.

8. White has sixteen pawn moves (there are eight pawns, and each can advance either one or two squares.)

HOMEWORK ANSWERS

1. King = K; Queen = Q; Rook = R; Bishop = B; Knight = N; Pawn = P.

2.

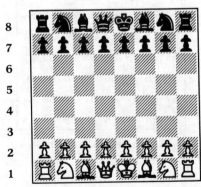

3. Each Knight is placed between a Rook and a Bishop (see Diagram 6).

4. One Bishop stands between the Queen

Lesson Two

Chess Notation

Review Questions:

1. Who moves first in a chess game?
2. What color is the left-hand corner square nearest a player?
3. How many pawns and pieces does White have in the starting position?
4. How many pawns does Black have in the initial position?
5. How many Knights does White have at the beginning of a game?

(Answers below)

Answers to Review Questions

1. White always makes the first move of a game.
2. Dark.
3. White has eight pieces and eight pawns in the starting position.
4. Eight pawns.
5. Two.

Chess Notation

The richness of chess today owes much to the many valuable contributions and ideas of our ancestors. One of the most interesting ideas was that of chess notation. The first chess book was written in Persia in 600 A.D.!

Today, nearly all countries accept the simple and convenient algebraic system of designating squares on the chessboard. In this system, each square on the board has a name which consists of one of the letters from **a** to **h** followed by a number from **1** to **8**. Diagrams 18 and 19 show all the squares and their names. Thus, the corner squares which the White Rooks always occupy in the initial position are **a1** and **h1**, while **a8** and **h8** indicate the location of the Black Rooks.

18

from White's side

19

from Black's side

Each vertical column of eight squares is called a "**file**." The files are designated by the first eight letters of the alphabet, a, b, c, d, e, f, g, and h, starting from the left on White's side. They are marked out in Diagram 20.

20

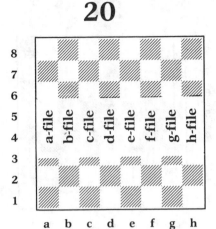

Each row of eight squares running across the board is called a "**rank**." They are designated by the numbers 1, 2, 3, 4, 5, 6, 7, and 8, starting from White's side. The ranks have been marked out in Diagram 21. Thus, in the initial position White's men are placed on the first and second ranks while Black's men are placed on the seventh and eighth ranks.

21

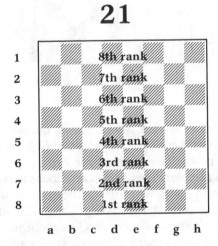

The board can also be divided into twenty-six diagonals varying in length from two to eight squares.

22

While any rank or file contains both light squares and dark squares, the squares making up any given diagonal are all of the same color, either light or dark. This can be seen in Diagram 23.

23

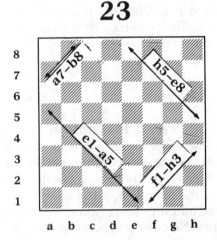

Diagonals are designated by the names of their end squares, for example the a1-h8 and the h1-a8 diagonals. These two diagonals, the only ones consisting of eight squares, are often called the long diagonals. They have been marked in Diagram 22 by the word

DIAGONAL

written across them. Diagonals which consist only of light squares, e.g. h5-e8 and f1-h3, are called light-square diagonals, while diagonals which consist only of dark squares, e.g. a7-b8 and e1-a5, are called dark-square diagonals. These diagonals are marked out in Diagram 23.

How To Write Down A Move

A move is playing a man from one square to another. The following conventional order is used in writing down a move:

1. Piece symbol
2. Square of departure
3. - (moves to) or x (captures on)
4. Square of arrival

You already know the symbols of all the chessmen (see Lesson 1). If there is no prefixing piece symbol, that means that the move is made by a pawn.

Here is an example: If the first move is made by the White pawn in front of the King, the pawn starts its move on e2 and finishes it on e4. The move should therefore be recorded as **1. e2-e4.** If Black replied to this move by pushing the pawn in front of his Queen two squares forward, that move would be written as **1. ... d7-d5** (the three dots mean that the move is made by Black. They are only used when writing Black's move alone, without White's move in front of it). If White on his second move captured the Black pawn on d5 with his pawn on e4, that would be written as **2. e4xd5.**

Pawn Promotion

Because of its limited mobility, a pawn is much weaker than any of the other men. However, it has a compensating quality: when it reaches the other end of the board, it can be changed into any piece of its own color, except the King. No other piece can be changed into anything else, no matter what square it reaches. A pawn moves very slowly, but if it gets to the opposite end of the board it can change into a powerful Queen! Diagram 24 shows how White pawns move towards the eighth rank, and in Diagram 25 you can see the progress of the Black pawns towards the first rank.

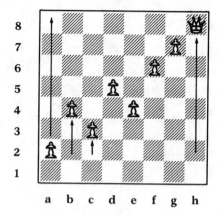

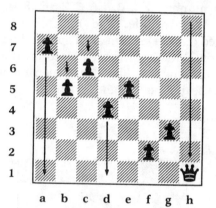

When a player's pawn reaches the last rank (eighth rank for White pawns and first rank for Black pawns), he can promote it to any piece of the same color. That is, he can choose between promoting a pawn to a Queen (the usual choice), a Rook, a Bishop, or a Knight. It doesn't matter if there is a Queen of the same color on the board already: you may have another one. When promoting a pawn to a Queen, chessplayers usually say, "I want a Queen," or just, "Queen!" It is possible for a player to have nine Queens; in practice, however, two should be enough. Similarly, the rules of the game allow a player to have ten Rooks, ten Bishops, or ten Knights, but there is no recorded instance of such cases ever occurring in a game of chess. If you cannot find an extra Queen, Rook, Bishop, or Knight in your set, use an upside-down Rook, spools of white or black thread, or some other suitable objects to represent the extra pieces.

Pawn promotion is compulsory. That is, a pawn reaching the last rank must be exchanged for a piece; it cannot remain a pawn. A pawn is promoted by removing the pawn from the board and placing the chosen piece on the promotion square.

The process of promoting or "Queening" a pawn is illustrated in Diagrams 26 and 27.

26

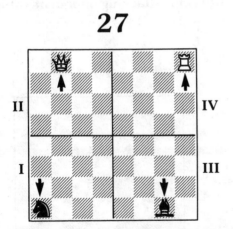

Promotion of a pawn: before the move.

27

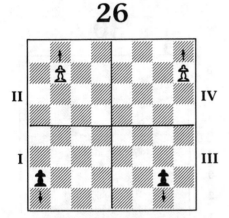

Promotion of a pawn: after the move.

The promotion square is sometimes called the "Queening square."

When a player has exchanged the pawn for a piece, his move is completed. Promotion of a pawn into any piece counts as one move. From his next move, the promoted piece (Queen, Rook, Bishop, or Knight) moves and captures in exactly the same way as a regular piece of that kind.

If a pawn has reached a square on the last rank by capturing an enemy piece on that square, the captured enemy piece is of course also removed from the board. See Diagrams 28 and 29.

28

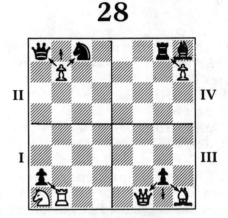

Promotion by capture:
How many different moves does the pawn have in each quarter?

29

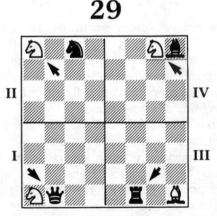

Promotion by capture: after the move.

When a pawn reaches the last rank, we must write down the symbol of the new piece after the usual notation of the move. In Diagrams 26-II and 27-II, we see White advancing his pawn from b7 to b8 and changing it to a Queen. This move is recorded as **b7-b8Q**. A pawn can also be changed into any piece if it reaches a square on the last rank by capturing an enemy piece on that square. The captured enemy piece is of course removed from the board. In Diagrams 28-II and 29-II you can see a White pawn on b7 capturing a Black Queen on a8 and becoming a Knight. This move is recorded as follows: **b7xa8N.**

It is clear that the possibility of promotion greatly increases the value of a pawn.

Now look at Diagram 28 and figure out how many different moves the pawn in each of the quarter diagrams can make.

Answers to Question about Diagram 28

In Quarter I the pawn has four different moves, since it can become four different pieces:

1. a2 x b1Q
1. a2 x b1R
1. a2 x b1B
1. a2 x b1N

In Quarter II the pawn has twelve different moves, in Quarter III it has twelve different moves, and in Quarter IV it has four different moves.

Recommendations

Do not try to memorize the diagrams, as they are only examples. Try rather to learn the ideas involved. You may never again come across the positions shown in the diagrams, but the ideas that they illustrate will repeat themselves many times in your games.

To understand the rest of the lessons properly, students must have a perfect knowledge of the designation of each square on the chessboard. See Diagrams 18 and 19. In practice, chessboards do not have the designations marked on them and every beginner should become capable as soon as possible of identifying the squares mentally. This is not so easy at first, especially for the Black player, since the squares are always numbered from White's side. In diagrams, White is always shown playing up the board and Black is shown playing down the board.

A useful device to help students memorize the board better is the well-known "Battleship Game," which is played as follows (See Diagrams 30 and 31). Two players each draw two chessboards. On one of them, the player marks the locations of his own ships. One square serves as a torpedo boat, two squares as a

cruiser, and three squares as a liner. This board is kept hidden from the opponent. On the other board, the player tries to search out his opponent's ships by "shooting" or "firing" at them. After each shot, the opponent has to say "hit" or "missed", and the player marks the square that he shot at as being either the location of an enemy ship or a blank spot, to remind him not to shoot at the same spot twice. The battle ends when one of the players has annihilated all his opponent's ships.

30

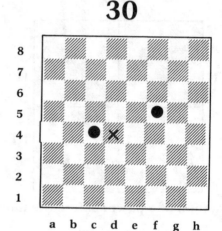

Battleship: attacking opponent's ships

31

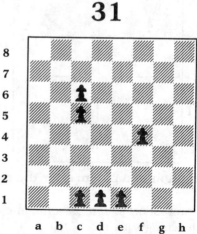

Battleship: location of own ships

The above game will help students to memorize the board in a very short time. Having a perfect knowledge of the chessboard not only helps a player to memorize positions better, but also improves his game: players who know the chessboard well rarely make mistakes. So, anyone who wants to develop his chessplaying skills should memorize the chessboard as soon as possible.

HOMEWORK
I. Diagrams 32 – 33
(Answers at the end)

32

	a	b	c	d	e	f	g	h	
8	7	24	53	36	5	22	51	34	8
7	54	37	6	23	52	35	4	21	7
6	25	8	55	38	45	12	33	50	6
5	38	59	46	13	48	57	20	3	5
4	9	26	15	56	11	44	49	32	4
3	60	39	10	47	14	31	2	19	3
2	27	16	41	62	29	18	43	64	2
1	40	61	28	17	42	63	30	1	1

Name the squares in their numeric order. Write your answer:

_____

_____

_____

33

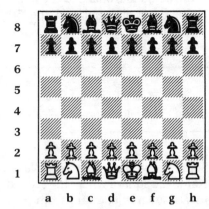

Name the squares on which the various White and Black men stand in the starting position. Write your answer:

Write your answer:

_____

_____

_____

II. Exercises
Write your answers in the spaces below.
1. Place the board as if you are White. Find the following squares: f7, a2, g3, e4, b5, and h6. What color are they? Write L for light or D for dark.

_____

_____

_____

2. Now place the board as if you are Black, and find these squares: g1, d3, c7, b1, h4, and b7. What color are they? Write L for light or D for dark.

_____

_____

_____

3. Which square is the intersection of:
the a1-h8 diagonal and the e-file?
the f1-a6 diagonal and the 5th
rank?

_____

_____

_____

4. Suppose you're playing Black.
Name the square where the second
row of squares (counting from your
side of the board) crosses the second file (counting from your left).

_____

_____

_____

5. Place eight pawns (four of each col-
or) on the board in such a way that
none of them can make a move or a
capture.

_____

_____

_____

6. Place the same eight pawns on the
board in such a way that each side
has six different possible captures.

_____

_____

_____

7. Learn to play the "Battleship
Game" (see Recommendations
and Diagrams 30 and 31).

Homework Answers
I. Diagrams 32-33

D-32 h1, g3, h5, g7, e8, c7, a8, b6, a4, c3,
e4, f6, d5, e3, c4, b2, d1, f2, h3, g5, h7, f8,
d7, b8, a6, b4, a2, c1, e2, g1, f3, h4, g6, h8,
f7, d8, b7, a5, b3, a1, c2, e1, g2, f4, e6, c5,
d3, e5, g4, h6, g8, e7, c8, a7, c6, d4, f5, d6,
b5, a3, b1, d2, f1, h2.

D-33
White: a1, a2, b1, b2, c1, c2, d1, d2, e1, e2,
f1, f2, g1, g2, h1, h2.

Black: a7, a8, b7, b8, c7, c8, d7, d8, e7, e8,
f7, f8, g7, g8, h7, h8.

II. Exercises

1. L, L, D, L, L, D.
2. D, L, D, L, D, L.
3. The a1-h8 diagonal crosses the
   e-file at e5; the f1-a6 diagonal
   crosses the fifth rank at b5.
4. g7.
5. White: a2, c2, e2, h2
   Black: a3, c3, e3, h3.
6. White: b4, c4, d4, e4.
   Black: b5, c5, d5, e5.

Lesson Three

How the Rook and Bishop Move and Capture

Check the homework of Lesson 2 (if necessary).

Review Questions:
1. Name the squares on which the White Bishops, Black Knights, Black Queen, and White King are located in the starting position.
2. How many Queens and Rooks are there on the board in the starting position?
3. Without looking at the board, name:
    (a) the diagonals that intersect at the d3 square;
    (b) the square where the b1-h7 and h5-e8 diagonals intersect;
    (c) the square where the second rank crosses the a1-h8 diagonal.
4. Suppose that you are playing Black. Name the square in the third row from you on the second file from the left.
5. Construct a position where a White pawn has a choice of four different moves.
6. Is it possible for White's a-pawn (the Queen's Rook Pawn) to wind up on the e-file? If so, how?

Answers to Review Questions:
1. At the start of the game, the White Bishops are on **c1** and **f1**, the Black Knights are on **b8** and **g8**, the Black Queen is on the dark square **d8**, and the White King is on **e1**.
2. At the start of the game there are two Queens (one White and one Black) and four Rooks (two White and two Black).
3. (a) **b1-h7** and **f1-a6**.
    (b) **g6**
    (c) **b2**
4. **g6**

5. There are of course many such positions. Here is an example. White pawn on **e2** and Black pawns on **d3** and **f3**. White to play has four different moves with his pawn (the pawn can capture either of the two Black pawns or move one or two squares ahead).
6. The a-pawn can reach the e-file by capturing four times.

The Center
By "center" we mean the four central squares d4, e4, d5, and e5. See Diagram 34. The importance of the center in chess will become clear later on.

34

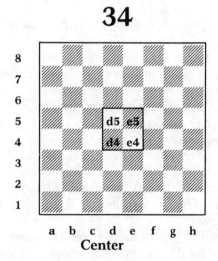

Center

How the Rook Moves and Captures
A Rook can move to any vacant square on the file or rank on which it stands, provided that no men of either color block the path. Diagrams 35 and 36 illustrate how it moves.

35

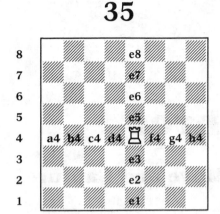

The Rook has 14 moves shown here.

36

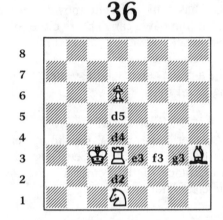

The Rook has 6 moves shown here.

It is clear that the Rook enjoys great freedom of action, as it is able to cross the entire board in a single move. However, although it can move in any direction, in any given move it can travel ony in one direction, i.e., it cannot change direction in the middle of a move. Thus, on an empty board, a Rook can reach any one of the 14 squares in a single move, see Diagram 35. It can reach any of the other squares in two moves, and can do so in two different ways.

Capturing is optional in chess. However, it is usually good to capture an enemy man since that will make the enemy's forces weaker than yours. As a result, his resistance will be weakened, and it will be much easier for you to win.

If a Rook moves to a square occupied by an enemy man, the latter is captured and re-

moved from the board at once. Diagrams 37–39 show how the Rook captures.

In Diagram 37, the Black Rook is attacking four White men. If it is Black's turn to play, he can capture any one of them.

37

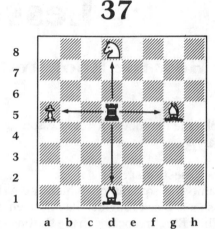

The Rook can capture the Bishop on d1 or g5, or Knight on d8, or pawn on a5.

Diagram 38 shows the resulting position if Black captures the White Bishop on g5, removing it from the board.

38

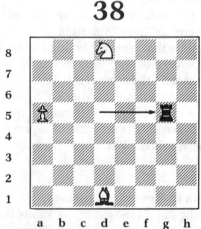

The Rook has captured the Bishop g5

In Diagram 39, the Black Rook is not attacking the White Bishop on a4, as there is a Black pawn in the way. Don't forget that the Rook cannot jump over men, whether its own or the opponent's. If the Black pawn in Diagram 39 is removed, then the Black Rook would be attacking the White Bishop on a4.

39

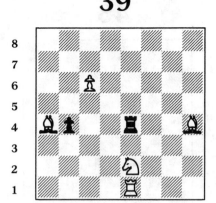

a b c d e f g h

The Black Rook can capture only the Bishop h4 or Knight, but not the pawn, Bishop a4, or Rook.

A man that attacks a square occupied by a friendly man (i.e., a man of its own color) is said to defend or protect it, since if an enemy man captures the friendly man, the defending man will in turn be able to capture the enemy man.

In Diagram 39, the Black Rook is attacking the White Knight, which is protected by the White Rook. If Black takes the Knight with his Rook, the White Rook can capture the Black Rook. Black would thus lose a Rook, and White would lose a Knight.

Diagram 40 shows some mini-positions that will help you to better understand the Rook, and also how chessmen move, attack, and defend each other in general.

40

Rooks move, attack, and defend
each other.

In 40-I, each Rook defends his partner and attacks an enemy Rook. In this situation, neither side can win a piece for nothing.

In 40-II, each side has a choice of three captures, and the side which moves first can win a Rook by any of those captures. Such situations occur when the four Rooks occupy the same rank or file.

In 40-III, each Rook defends its partner of the same color, and none of the Rooks are attacked.

In 40-IV, none of the Rooks attack or defend any of the other Rooks.

If a man is captured and a similar man has been given up for it (a Bishop for a Bishop, a Rook for a Rook, etc.), there has been no loss to either side. This is known as a trade, or, more exactly, an even trade.

How the Bishop Moves and Captures

The Bishop always moves diagonally, along squares of the same color (Diagrams 41 and 42). It can move in any direction, but in any one move it can move in only one direction: i.e., it cannot change direction during a move. Each player has two Bishops at the start of a game, one standing on a light square and the other on a dark square. The Bishop which stands on a light square at the beginning of the game can never move to a dark square, and similarly, the Bishop on a dark square at the start of the game can never move to a light square. The Bishop that moves only on light squares is called the light-square Bishop and the one that moves only on dark squares is called the dark-square Bishop. A Bishop can move to any vacant square on either of the diagonals (Diagram 41) on which it stands, so long as there are no men of either color blocking the way (Diagram 42).

It is obvious that the Bishop has great mobility when there are no obstructions. It can cross the board in a single move. The Bishop controls 13 squares from a central square and 7 squares from a square on the edge.

41

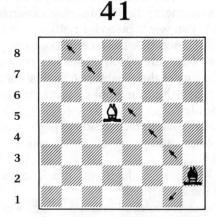

Bishop d5 has 13 moves, and Bishop h2 has 7 moves.

Since the Bishop can only move on squares of one color, enemy men on squares of the other color are immune to attack by it.

42

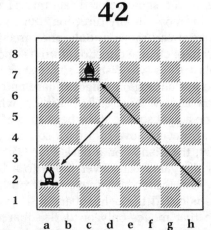

Light-square Bishop moved to a2, dark-square Bishop moved to c7.

If a Bishop moves to a square occupied by an enemy man, the latter is captured and removed from the board at once. See Diagram 43, which shows how the Bishop captures.

43

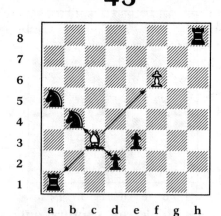

The Bishop can capture the Rook a1, Knight b4, or pawn d2, but not Knight a5 or Rook h8.

In the position in the diagram, the White Bishop can capture the Ra1, Nb4 or Pd2. Since Bishops cannot jump over enemy men, the White Bishop in the diagram cannot capture the Na5, and it cannot capture the Rh8 since Bishops are not allowed to jump over their own men either.

The Pd2 in Diagram 43 is protected by the Pe3, so if the White Bishop captures the Pd2, Black can take the Bishop with his Pe3! White would lose a Bishop, and Black would lose a pawn.

Diagram 44 shows the resulting position if White captures the Nb4 in Diagram 43.

44

The Bishop had captured the Knight b4

Diagram 45 shows a position where White's light-square Bishop prevents the advance of five Black pawns situated on black squares. If Black moves his pawns, the White Bishop will capture all of them in five moves. We can conclude therefore that a Bishop is stronger than a pawn, but weaker than a Rook, since a Rook can move on squares of both colors.

45

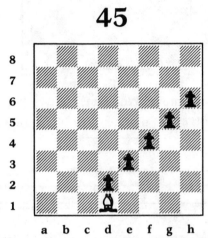

a b c d e f g h

Diagonal d1-h5 is controlled by the Bishop, and all five Black pawns perish.

However, in exceptional cases a pawn can turn out to be stronger than a Bishop. For example, in Diagram 46 the White pawn on a2 can advance to its queening square without being hindered by the Black Bishop, which is blocked in by its own pawns.

46

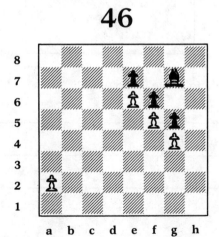

a b c d e f g h

Black pawns block their Bishop and the Bishop cannot stop the White pawn on a2.

Recommendations

You already know how to play chess with pawns alone. Now that you have learned how the Rook and the Bishop move, you are to play chess using these two pieces as well as pawns!

To begin with, set up the Rooks, Bishops and pawns in the positions they would occupy in an actual full-scale game of chess (see Diagram 47).

47

a b c d e f g h

Now play according to the following rules:

1. A pawn that reaches the other end of the board can and must be promoted into either a Bishop or a Rook, after which the game continues.

2. You win the game:
   (a) if your opponent gives up;
   (b) if you are the first to capture all your opponent's pieces and pawns; or
   (c) if after one of your moves all your opponent's pieces and pawns are blocked and do not have any moves, while at least one of your own pieces or pawns can make at least one move.

3. A game is a draw (tie game):
   (a) if the players agree to call it a draw;
   (b) if both players' pieces and pawns are blocked and neither side can make a move; or
   (c) if fifty (50) consecutive moves go by without either side having moved a pawn or captured a man.

48

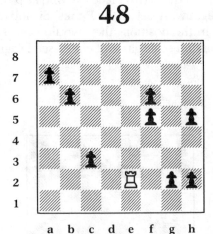

What is the minimum number of moves the White Rook needs to capture all Black pawns, provided the Black pawns do not move?

_____

_____

_____

49

What is the minimum number of moves the White Bishop needs to capture all Black pawns? Assume the Black pawns do not move.

_____

_____

_____

50

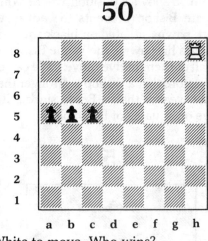

White to move. Who wins?

_____

_____

_____

51

White to move. Who wins?

_____

_____

_____

52

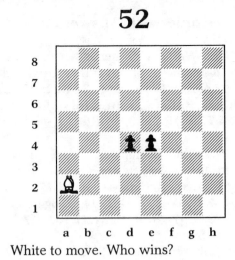

White to move. Who wins?

_____

_____

_____

53

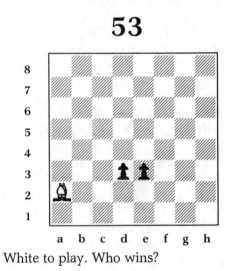

White to play. Who wins?

_____

_____

_____

54

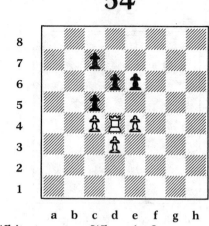

White to move. Who wins?

_____

_____

_____

55

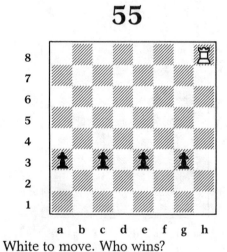

White to move. Who wins?

_____

_____

_____

56

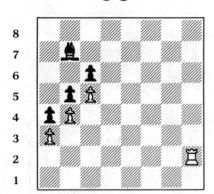

White to play. Who wins?

_____

_____

_____

57

White to play. Can he win?

_____

_____

_____

Remember: a clear and exact mental image of each square of the chessboard is a guarantee of mastering further material. You should prove it to yourself before going further.

Homework Answers

D-48 The White Rook needs ten moves to capture all the Black pawns if they are not allowed to move: **1. Re2xg2, 2. Rg2xh2, 3. Rh2xh5, 4. Rh5xf5, 5. Rf5xf6, 6. Rf6xb6, 7. Rb6-b7, 8. Rb7xa7, 9. Ra7-c7, and 10. Rc7xc3.**

D-49 The White Bishop needs eleven moves to capture all the Black pawns if they are not allowed to move: **1. Bc6xb7, 2. Bb7xa6, 3. Ba6xc4, 4. Bc4xe2, 5. Be2xg4, 6. Bg4-f5, 7. Bf5xh7, 8. Bh7-g8, 9. Bg8xf7, 10. Bf7-e8, and 11. Be8xa4.**

D-50 White wins with **1. Rh8-h5 b5-b4 2. Rh5xc5 a5-a4 3. Rc5-c4 b4-b3 4. Rc4xa4 b3-b2 5. Ra4-b4 b2-b1Q 6. Rb4xb1.** Other solutions are also possible.

D-51 White loses, as one of the Black pawns will reach the first rank safely: **1. Rh8-h4 b4-b3 2. Rh4xc4 b3-b2 3. Rc4-b4 a4-a3 4. Rb4-b3 a3-a2**, and so on.

D-52 White can win by playing **1. Ba2-d5.** If Black replies with **1. ... e4-e3,** then White plays **2. Bd5-c4** and the Black pawns must perish. If you study the position carefully, you will see that White will win after any starting move except **1. Ba2-b1.**

D-53 No matter what White plays, Black can win by replying with **1. ... e3-e2,** and the Black e-pawn will become a Rook or Bishop on the next move.

D-54 White wins with **1. Rd4-d5 e6-e5 2. d3-d4 e5xd4 3. Rd5-h5 d4-d3 4. Rh5-h3 d3-d2 5. Rh3-d3** and so on, or **1. Rd4-d5 e6xd5 2. e4xd5 c7-c6 3. d5xc6 d6-d5 4. c4xd5 c5-c4 4. d3xc4.**

D-55 White wins with **1. Rh8-h1.** All the Black pawns will be captured as soon as they reach the first rank.

D-56 White wins as the Black Bishop is in a corner and has very few squares (only three) to which it can move. The White Rook controls these squares and then captures the Bishop: **1. Rh2-h8 Bb7-a6 2. Rh8-b8** and captures the Bishop on the next move.

D-57 The position is a draw here since there the Black Bishop has many squares to move to and can protect its pawns from the White Rook.

Lesson Four

How the Queen and Knight Move and Capture

Check Lesson Three Homework if necessary.

Review Questions:

1. Name the square where the third rank crosses the b1-h7 diagonal.
2. Without looking at a chessboard, name the White and Black men and the squares they stand on at the start of the game.
3. Can the White a-pawn (the Queen's Rook Pawn) wind up on the f-file during a game? If so, how?
4. Can a situation with Black pawns on a2, a3, a4, and a5 occur in a game?
5. Without looking at the board, say where the mobility of a Bishop is greater — in the center or in a corner?
6. Without looking at the board, name the maximum number of squares that could be needed by a Rook to get from one square of an empty board to another.
7. Without looking at the board, determine how many moves are needed for a Bishop on a1 to reach h2 on an empty board. How many moves does it need to get from a1 to h6?
8. Which Bishops can never collide?

Answers:

1. d3.
2. White: Ke1, Qd1, Ra1, Rh1, Nb1, Ng1, Bc1, Bf1, P's a2, b2, c2, d2, e2, f2, g2, h2; Black: Ke8, Qd8, Ra8, Rh8, Nb8, Ng8, Bc8, Bf8, P's a7, b7, c7, d7, e7, f7, g7, h7.
3. The White a-pawn can reach the f-file by capturing five times, e.g., **a2 x b3 x c4 x d5 x e6 x f7.**
4. Yes. The pawn on a4 could have got there in one move from b5 by the capture ... **b5 x a4**; the pawn on a3 could have got there in two moves from c5 by the captures ...

c5 x b4 and ... **b4 x a3**; and the pawn on a2 could have got there in three moves by the captures ... **d5 x c4, ... c4 x b3,** and ... **b3 x a2.** Thus a total of six capturing moves would be needed.

5. A Bishop has 13 moves in the center of the board and only 7 in a corner.
6. Two moves.
7. Two moves to reach h2: **Ba1-e5-h2** and two to reach h6: **Ba1-g7-h6.**
8. Bishops that move on light squares never meet the Bishops that move on dark squares.

How The Queen Moves and Captures

The Queen is the most powerful piece in chess. In appearance, it is taller than any of the other pieces except the King. The Queen combines the moves of the Rook and the Bishop. It can move in any direction (but it cannot change direction in the middle of a move) along the entire length of any rank, file, or diagonal on which it stands, if there are no obstacles in its way. Diagram 58 shows a position in which the Queen controls a total of 27 squares.

58

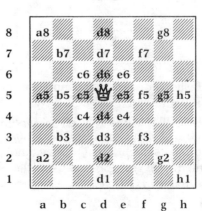

Diagram 59 illustrates one possible move that the Queen in Diagram 58 could make. On the edge of the board the Queen is weaker, as it has only 21 possible moves.

59

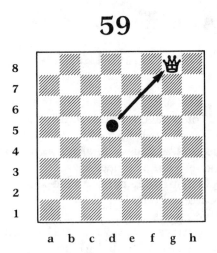

The Queen can have two types of obstacles in its way: friendly men, which cannot be displaced or jumped over, and enemy men, which can be captured and removed from the board. This will become clearer when we examine Diagram 60.

60

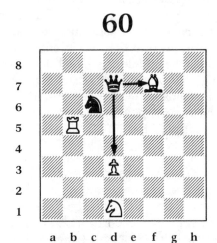

The Black Queen there can capture the White Bishop or pawn, but cannot capture the White Knight, which is blocked by the White pawn and thus is safe. The White Rook too is safe, as the Queen's own Knight stands in the way. For all its might, the Queen cannot jump over men. Diagram 61 shows the Black Queen's move ... **Qd7xf7**, capturing the White Bishop.

61

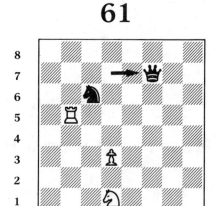

Diagram 62 shows a position where the Black Queen can capture any one of eight White men, while the Queen itself is not under attack by any of them.

62

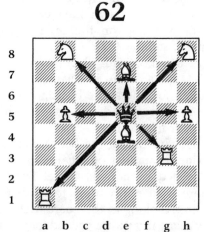

The position in Diagram 63 is another illustration of the Queen's might. By moving **Qb5-g5**, White can attack six Black men simultaneously, although it can only capture one of them on its next move.

63

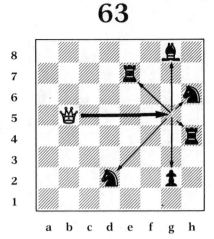

How the Knight Moves and Captures

Knights have always ridden horses. That is why a Knight in chess has the shape of a horse's head.

The Knight's move is illustrated in Diagram 64, where the Knight on d4 controls the squares c6, e6, f5, f3, e2, c2, b3 and b5.

64

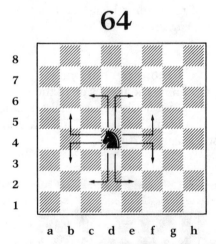

It is clear that a Knight's move in any direction has the shape of a capital L. Good descriptions of the Knight's move are:

a) two squares sideways, then one square up or down;

b) two squares up or down, then one square sideways.

Either of these descriptions can be used to describe any Knight's move.

Diagram 65 shows one of the eight possible moves of a Knight on the central square d4: **Nd4-f3.**

65

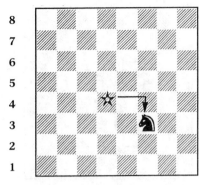

Note that a Knight changes the color of its square every time it moves. Thus, starting from the dark square d4 (Diagram 64), it moves to the light square f3 (Diagram 65).

Diagram 66 shows the following Knight's moves: **Na8-b6, ... Nb2-a4, Nf6-h5 and ... Ng1-e2.**

66

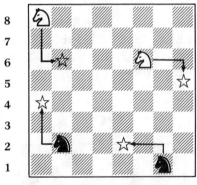

A Knight is not allowed to move just one square or two squares and then stop. A Knight in a corner has only two moves.

Like any good horseman, the chess Knight too is able to jump over obstacles. The Knight is the only chess piece with the power to jump over its own and enemy men. Unlike checkers, however, the Knight never captures the men it jumps over. Diagram 67 shows a White Knight on d4 that is surrounded by its own and enemy men.

67

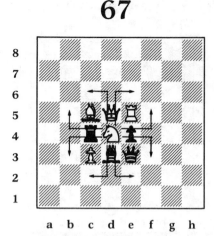

It may jump over any of these men and has a choice of eight different moves, just as it does on the empty board in Diagram 64. If the Knight's destination is occupied by an enemy man, the latter is captured by the Knight. The enemy man is removed from the board and the Knight takes its place instead. Knights operate well in close quarters. A Knight is able to jump into the middle of things and, if it feels uncomfortable there, it can leap right out again.

In Diagram 68, the White Knight can capture the Black Bishop on b3 (**Na1xb3**). This Knight cannot move to c2, since there is already another Knight there.

68

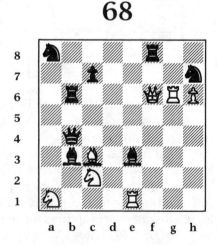

The Knight on c2 is much stronger than the Knight on a1, as it has a choice of four different moves: **Nc2-a3, Nc2-d4,** capturing the Queen by **Nc2xb4** (see Diagram 69), and capturing the Bishop on e3 by **Nc2 x e3.**

69

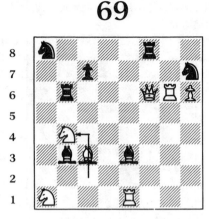

However, it cannot go to a1 or e1, since these squares are occupied by friendly pieces. The Black Knight on a8 has no moves at all, since the squares b6 and c7 are occupied by Black pieces. The Black Knight on h7 can move to g5 (**Nh7-g5**) or capture the White Queen (**Nh7-f6**). It cannot go to f8, since that square is occupied by a friendly piece, a Black Rook.

A Knight's strength is approximately equal to that of a Bishop. A Knight is stronger than a pawn, but weaker than a Rook or a Queen.

Place a Knight on a board and move it as shown in Diagrams 64–66.

Recommendations

You now know the moves of all the men except the King. Set up these men in the positions they would occupy in an actual full-scale chess game (see Diagram 70).

70

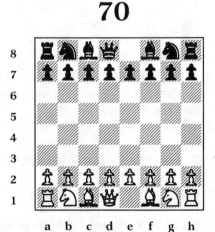

Start playing from this position. The rules are the same as in the Rook, Bishop and Pawn game of Lesson Three, except for Rule 1. The new Rule 1 is:

1. A pawn that reaches the other end of the board can and must be promoted into a Queen, Rook, Bishop, or Knight, after which the game continues.

a) How many possiblities has the White Knight to capture?

b) In how many moves will the White Knight capture all the Black pieces, provided that Black does not move?

_____

_____

_____

HOMEWORK
I. Diagrams 71–80
(Answers at the end)

71

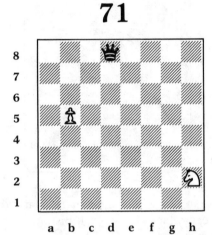

Black to move. Find a square from which the Queen attacks the White Knight and the pawn simultaneously.

_____

_____

_____

73

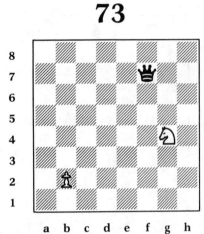

Black to move. Find the square from which the Black Queen attacks the White Knight and the pawn simultaneously.

_____

_____

_____

72

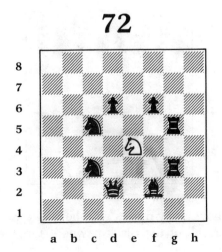

74

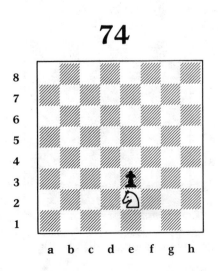

In how many moves will the White Knight capture the Black pawn, provided the pawn doesn't move?

_____

_____

_____

75

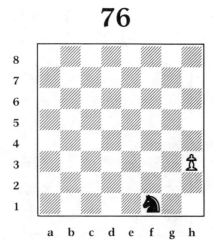

White to play. Find the square from which the Queen attacks the Black Knight and the Bishop simultaneously.

_____

_____

_____

76

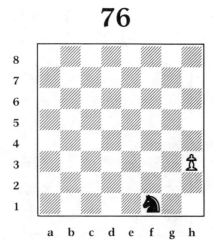

In how many moves will the Black Knight

capture the White pawn if the pawn doesn't move?

_____

_____

_____

77

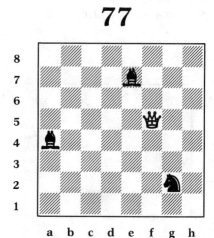

White to play. Find the square from which the Queen attacks both Black Bishops and the Knight.

_____

_____

_____

78

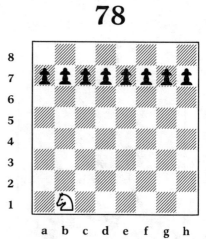

In how many moves will the White Knight capture all of the Black pawns if they don't

28

move?

_____

_____

_____

79

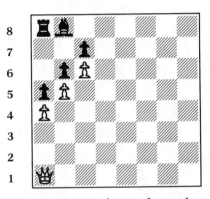

White to play and win.

_____

_____

_____

80

	a	b	c	d	e	f	g	h
8	31	54	47	8	33	10	27	50
7	46	7	32	53	28	49	34	11
6	5	30	55	48	9	36	51	26
5	56	45	6	29	52	25	12	35
4	43	4	57	20	61	14	37	24
3	58	19	44	1	40	23	62	13
2	3	42	17	60	21	64	15	38
1	18	59	2	41	16	39	22	63

The numbers show the order in which a Knight moves from square to square in making a "Knight's Tour" of the chessboard.

a) In the same order, write down the names of the squares in chess notation.

In a Knight's Tour, a Knight lands on every square of the board without landing on any square twice. Mathematicians have calculated that there are more than 30 million different Knight's Tours possible. Diagram 80 shows just one of them

b) Add up the number of the squares on each rank and on each file and compare them!

Homework Answers

D-71 1. ... Qd8-b8 attacks the White Knight and pawn at the same time.

D-72 a) The White Knight has a choice of eight different captures: Ne4xd6, Ne4xf6, Ne4xg5, Ne4xg3, Ne4xf2, Ne4xd2, Ne4xc3, and Ne4xc5.

b) If the Black pieces do not move, the White Knight can capture them all in fifteen moves: 1. Ne4xd2, 2. Nd2-e4, 3. Ne4xc3, 4. Nc3-e4, 5. Ne4xc5, 6. Nc5-e4, 7. Ne4xd6, 8. Nd6-e4, 9. Ne4xf6, 10. Nf6-e4, 11. Ne4xg5, 12. Ng5-e4, 13. Ne4xg3, 14. Ng3-e4, and 15. Ne4xf2.

D-73 1. ... Qf7-g7 attacks the White Knight and the pawn at the same time.

D-74 If the Black pawn doesn't move, the White Knight can capture it in three moves: 1. Ne2-c3, 2. Nc3-d5, and 3. Nd5xe3.

D-75 1. Qb6-d8 and 1. Qb6-e3 both attack the Black Knight and Bishop simultaneously.

D-76 If the White pawn doesn't move, the Black Knight can capture it in four moves: 1. ... Nf1-d2, 2. ... Nd2-e4, 3. ... Ne4-f2, and 4. ... Nf2xh3.

D-77 The White Queen attacks the Black Knight and both Black Bishops with the move 1. Qf5-e4.

D-78 If the Black pawns don't move, the White Knight can capture all of them in 18 moves: 1. Nb1-c3, 2. Nc3-b5, 3. Nb5xa7, 4. Na7-b5, 5. Nb5xc7, 6. Nc7-d5, 7. Nd5xe7, 8. Ne7-f5, 9. Nf5xg7, 10. Ng7-h5, 11. Nh5-f6, 12. Nf6xh7, 13. Nh7-g5, 14. Ng5xf7, 15. Nf7-e5, 16. Ne5xd7, 17. Nd7-c5, and 18. Nc5xb7.

D-79 1. Qa1-h8. The White Queen will capture the Black pieces, which are boxed in the corner.

D-80 **a)** 1. d3, 2. c1, 3. a2, 4. b4, 5. a6 6. c5, 7. b7, 8. d8, 9. e6, 10. f8, 11. h7, 12. g5, 13. h3, 14. f4, 15. g2, 16. e1, 17. c2, 18. a1, 19. b3, 20. d4, 21. e2, 22. g1, 23. f3, 24. h4, 25. f5, 26. h6, 27. g8, 28. e7, 29. d5, 30. b6, 31. a8, 32. c7, 33. e8, 34. g7, 35. h5, 36. f6, 37. g4, 38. h2, 39. f1, 40. e3, 41. d1, 42. b2, 43. a4, 44. c3, 45. b5, 46. a7, 47. c8, 48. d6, 49. f7, 50. h8, 51. g6, 52. e5, 53. d7, 54. b8, 55. c6, 56. a5, 57. c4, 58. a3, 59. b1, 60. d2, 61. e4, 62. g3, 63. h1, and 64. f2.

      b) The numbers in any file or rank add up to 260.

Lesson Five

How the King Moves and Captures. Check. Checkmate.

Check Lesson 4 homework if necessary.

Review Questions
1. Which men always attack an enemy man in such a way that the enemy man cannot be saved by a man being interposed between it and the attacking man?
2. Which piece can be moved in the starting position before any pawns are moved?
3. How many squares are there on the board from which the Knight can make only two moves?
4. Without looking at a board, count up how many different moves can be made by White and Black in the starting position.
5. Without looking at a board, say where the mobility of the Queen is greater — in the center or in a corner.
6. How many men can a Queen attack simultaneously?
7. Without looking at a board, say whether each of the following squares is dark or light: b2, d3, e7, f4, h3.
8. Without looking at a board, name all the squares on the h2-b8 and the h1-a8 diagonals.

Answers to Review Questions

1. The pawn and the Knight.
2. The Knight, because it can jump over the pawns.
3. The four corners: a1, a8, h1, and h8.
4. White and Black can each begin the game with twenty different moves (16 pawn moves and four Knight moves).
5. The Queen is stronger in the center, where it has 27 moves, compared to only 21 in a corner.
6. The Queen can attack eight men simultaneously.
7. b2-D, d3-L, e7-D, f4-D, h3-L.
8. The h2-b8 diagonal consists of the dark squares h2, g3, f4, e5, d6, c7, and b8, while the h1-a8 diagonal consists of the light squares h1, g2, f3, e4, d5, c6, b7, and a8.

How The King Moves and Captures

The King is the most important piece in chess, the heart and soul of the game. If you lose any other piece except the King, you can still play on. If you lose your King, however, you lose the game.

The King moves like the Queen, but only one square at a time. Thus, it can move forwards, backwards, sideways, or diagonally.

Diagram 81 illustrates the King's moves.

81

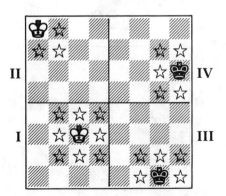

In 81-I, the King controls eight squares, as it always does except when it is on the edge of the board. 81-III and 81-IV show that on the edge the King has only five moves, while 81-II shows that in a corner the King's mobility is restricted even more, to only three squares.

Like all chessmen except the Knight, the King cannot jump over other men or move onto a square occupied by a man of its own color. Thus, in 82-I, the King can move to b2, b4, d2, and d4, but not to the squares occupied by the White pawns.

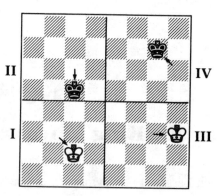

82

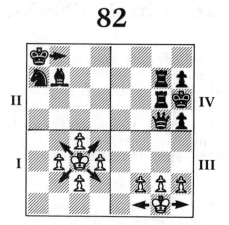

Similarly, the Black King in 82-II has only one move, to b8, while the White King in 82-III can move only to f1 or h1. In 82-IV, the Black King is completely surrounded by its own pieces and thus has no moves at all.

The King captures the same way as it moves. Diagrams 83 and 84 illustrate how the King captures by showing positions before a capture has been made (see Diagram 83).

83

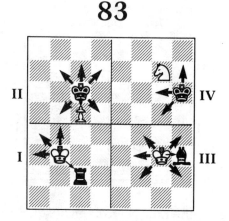

and after a capture has been made (see Diagram 84).

Capturing means taking the opponent's man off the board and moving your man onto the square the opponent's man occupied. Note that capturing is **not** compulsory in chess.

Check

When the King is attacked by an enemy piece, it is said to be "in check." A basic rule of chess is that whenever a player's King is put into check, the player must immediately, on the very next move, get his King out of check. In keeping with this, a King is never allowed to move into check either. That is, a King must never be moved onto a square where it will be within the capturing range of an enemy piece. It follows from this that neither King can put the other into check, and hence the two Kings can never stand on adjacent squares. Nor can a King capture a defended enemy piece, since it would thereby be moving into check. If by mistake a King has been left in check or moved into check, then as soon as the mistake is found out, the position before the King was left in check or moved into check must be set up and another move must be made. Checking is not obligatory, nor is it in itself either good or bad. Many beginners try to check whenever possible simply because they like announcing "check!".

In Diagram 85-I, Black has just moved his Knight (**Nd2-b3**) and put White's King in check. The Knight is directly attacking the White King, who must try to get out of check. 85-II to 85-IV show other examples of check.

85

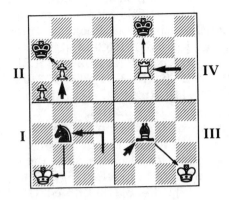

How To Get Out Of Check

There are three different ways to get out of check:

1. By moving your King to a safe square which is not attacked by any enemy man;
2. by moving one of your own men between your King and the checking piece;
3. by capturing the piece which is checking your King.

The King is in check in each of the four positions shown in Diagram 86, but in each case it has five different ways of getting out of check.

86

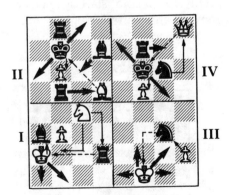

Checkmate

If none of the three ways of getting out of check are possible, then your King is said to be **checkmated** and you lose the game.

A King can be checkmated by any enemy piece except the other King.

Diagrams 87–92 show positions where the King is checkmated. Make sure that in each case you understand why it is checkmated.

87

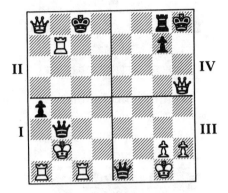

Queen checkmates

88

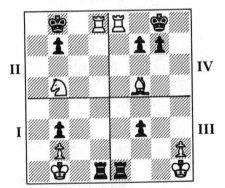

Rook checkmates

89

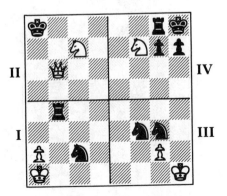

Knight checkmates

90

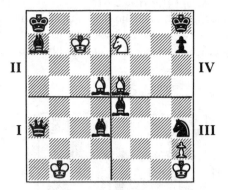

Bishop checkmates

91

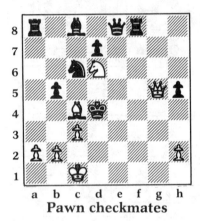

Pawn checkmates

Diagram 92 is a problem where White is to play and checkmate the Black King in one move. There are 47 different ways of doing this.

A move of the Rook on b2 opens up the diagonal of the Bishop on a1, which checkmates the White King. This accounts for fourteen checkmates, since the Rook can move to fourteen squares: (1) **Rb2-a2**, (2) **Rb2-c2**, (3) **Rb2-d2**, (4) **Rb2-e2**, (5) **Rb2-f2**, (6) **Rb2-g2**, (7) **Rb2-h2**, (8) **Rb2-b1**, (9) **Rb2-b3**, (10) **Rb2-b4**, (11) **Rb2-b5**, (12) **Rb2-b6**, (13) **Rb2-b7**, and (14) **Rb2xb8**.

A move of the Bishop on d5 allows the Queen on c5 to checkmate the Black King. This accounts for 11 mates, since the Bishop on d5 can make 11 moves: (15) **Bd5-a8**, (16) **Bd5-b7**, (17) **Bd5-c6**, (18) **Bd5-e4**, (19) **Bd5-f3**, (20) **Bd5-g2**, (21) **Bd5-h1**, (22) **Bd5-a2**, (23) **Bd5-b3**, (24) **Bd5-c4**, and (25) **Bd5-e6**.

A move of the Knight on f5 allows the Rook on g5 to checkmate the Black King. This accounts for seven checkmates: (26) **Nf5-e3**, (27) **Nf5-d4**, (28) **Nf5-d6**, (29) **Nf5-e7**, (30) **Nf5-g7**, (31) **Nf5-h6**, and (32) **Nf5-h4**.

The White Queen can make six moves which checkmate the Black King: (33) **Qc5-c3**, (34) **Qc5-c7**, (35) **Qc5-d4**, (36) **Qc5-d6**, (37) **Qc5-e3**, and (38) **Qc5-e7**.

And, finally, there are nine different pawn moves which checkmate the Black King: (39) **a7xb8 = Q**, (40) **a7xb8 = B**, (41) **d7xe8 = Q**, (42) **d7xe8 = R**, (43) **f7xe8 = Q**, (44) **f7xe8 = R**, (45) **h7-h8 = Q**, (46) **h7-h8 = B**, and (47) **d3-d4**.

Recommendations

Now that you know how all the men move, set them up in the starting position (see Diagram 93) and start playing!

92

93

Don't forget that to win you have to checkmate your opponent's King, not capture all his men. The goal of any real chess game is to checkmate the opponent's King. Don't make your moves in a big hurry. Take your time. It is better to play one good game, taking the time to think, than ten poor ones in a rush.

HOMEWORK
Diagrams 94–103
(Answers at the end)

94

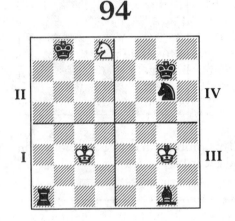

Can the King capture a piece in each quarter?

_____

_____

_____

95

Record all possible moves by the King in

each quarter.

_____

_____

_____

96

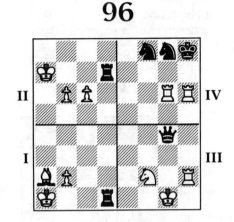

Record all possible moves which protect the King in each quarter from check.

_____

_____

_____

97

Record all possible moves which protect the King in each quarter from check.

In Diagrams 98–101, White is to move and checkmate in one move.

Write down your answers in the space provided.

98

100

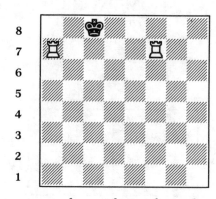

This problem has two solutions. Find them and record.

99

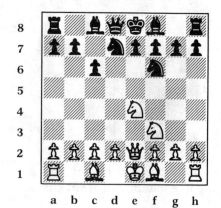

101

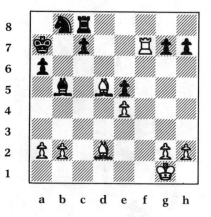

102

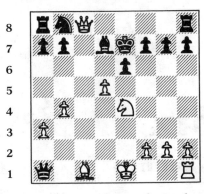

White to play. Checkmate in one move.

_____

_____

_____

103

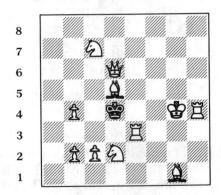

This problem has 43 solutions. Find them and record.

_____

_____

_____

_____

_____

_____

HOMEWORK ANSWERS

D-94   In I, II, and III, the King cannot capture the enemy pieces as they are too far away — a King can only move one square at a time. The King in IV cannot capture the Knight next to it since it is of the same color, and capturing your own men is not allowed in chess.

D-95   The King can only move as follows:
In I: **1. Kc2xb1** (only one move)
In II: **1. Kb6-a5; 1. Kb6-a7; 1. Kb6xc7** (three moves)
In III: **1. Kh3-h4; 1. Kh3-g4** (two moves)
In IV: **1. Kh7-g6** (only one move)

D-96   The King can get out of check by:
I: **1. Ba2-b1** (only one move)
II: **1. Ka7-a8; 1. Ka7-b8; 1. Ka7-a6; 1. b6-b7; 1. c6-c7; 1. c6xd7** (six moves)
III: **1. Kg1-f1; 1. Kg1-h1; 1. Nf2xg4; 1. Rh2-g2** (four moves)
IV: **1. ... Nf8-h7; 1. ... Ng8xh6** (two moves)

D-97   The King can get out of check by:
I: **1. Bc2xa4** (only one move)
II. **1. ... Kb6xc5; 1. ... Kb6-a6** (two moves)
III. **1. Ng1-f3; 1. Kh1-h2** (two moves)
IV. **1. ... Kf7-e6; 1. ... Kf7-e7; 1. ... Kf7-f8; 1. ... Kf7-g8; 1. ... Nf6xh5; 1. ... g7-g6** (six moves)

D-98   **1. Qd5xf7 checkmate**

D-99   **1. Ne4-d6 checkmate**

D-100   **1. Ra7-a8 or 1. Rf7-f8 checkmates**

D-101   **1. Bd2-e3 checkmate**

D-102   **1. d5-d6 checkmate**

D-103   1–6: **Kg4-f5/g5/h5/f3/g3/h3.** Each of these six King moves allows the Rook on h4 to checkmate.

7–11: **Qd6-c5/b6/e5/f4/f6.** Five checkmates with the Queen.

12–25: **Re3-a3/b3/c3/d3/f3/g3/h3/e1/e2/e4/e5/e6/e7/e8.** Fourteen checkmates by the Bg1 resulting from the moves of the Re3.

26–38: **Bd5-a2/b3/c4/e6/f7/g8/a8/b7/c6/e4/f3/g2/h1.** Thirteen checkmates by the Qd6 resulting from moves of the Bd5.

39–40: **Nd2-b3/f3.** Two checkmates by the Nd2.

41–42: **Nc7-b5/e6.** Two checkmates by the Nc7.

43: **c2-c3.** One checkmate by the pawn c2.

Total: 6 + 5 + 14 + 13 + 2 + 2 + 1 = 43 possible checkmates!

Lesson Six

En Passant Pawn Captures

Check homework (if necessary).

Review Questions

1. What piece can attack a Queen without itself being attacked by the Queen?
2. Where can a King trap a Knight in such a way that the Knight cannot avoid being captured?
3. How many moves does a Knight need to get from g1 to f1? Name the route.
4. How many moves does a Rook need to get from b1 to h7 on an empty board?
5. Why cannot a King stand next to the opponent's King?
6. Is it possible to checkmate the opponent by a King's move?
7. Is it possible to checkmate the White King and the Black King simultaneously?
8. Record all the moves by which the White Queen can check the Black King in Diagram 104.

Answers to Review Questions:

1. The Knight.
2. The King can trap a Knight in a corner. For example, in Diagram 105, wherever the Black Knight moves it will be captured by the King, while if it does not move, White will play **Kc6-b7** and capture the Knight the next move.

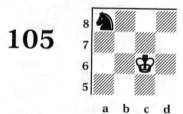

3. A Knight needs three moves to get from g1 to f1: e.g., **1. Ng1-e2, 2. Ne2-g3, 3. Ng3-f1.** The Knight can also get to f1 in three moves via f3 and d2 or via f3 and h2.
4. A Rook needs two moves to get from b1 to f7: **1. Rb1-f1 2. Rf1-f7, or 1. Rb1-b7 2. Rb7-f7.**
5. Because a King is not allowed to move into check, as it would be doing if it moved next to the other King.
6. Yes. For example, in Diagram 106 White can give checkmate with the Rook on h1 by the King move **1. Kh2-g1.**

106

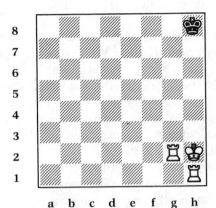

7. No. The players in a game of chess must move by turns, and as soon as one King is checkmated the game is over, and the player whose King has been checkmated is not allowed to make a reply, even if it would checkmate his opponent's King.

8. There are eight different moves by which the White Queen can check the Black King. These are: **1. Qg3-b3, 2. Qg3-d3, 3. Qg3-f3, 4. Qg3-g2, 5. Qg3-g5, 6. Qg3-g8, 7. Qg3-d6, 8. Qg3-e5.** Note that the last two checks are not good since the Black King can capture the White Queen.

En Passant Pawn Captures

You will remember that every pawn, the first time it moves, and only then, has the option of moving two squares forward instead of just one. You will also remember that pawns capture diagonally, and not the way they move. Keeping these facts in mind, look at the following diagrams and learn one final rule — a special pawn move.

107

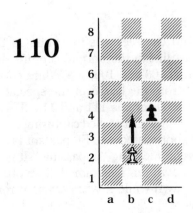

Pawn move: 1. b2-b3

Diagrams 107 and 110 show a White pawn on b2 and a Black pawn on c4. If the White pawn moves one square forward on its first move, the position in Diagram 108 will occur.

108

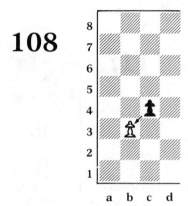

Here the Black pawn on c4 can capture the White pawn on b3, and if it does so, the position will be as in Diagram 109.

109

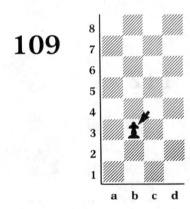

110

If the White pawn shown in Diagram 107 or 110 moves forward **two** squares on its first move, the resulting position will be as shown in Diagram 111, and the White pawn seems to have escaped being captured.

111

8
7
6
5
4
3
2
1

a b c d

However, a special rule allows the Black pawn to capture the White pawn as if it had only moved one square. The resulting position is shown in Diagram 112.

112

8
7
6
5
4
3
2
1

a b c d

As you can see, it is the same as Diagram 109. Just like in the normal capture shown in Diagrams 108 and 109, the White pawn is removed from the board in the special capture shown in Diagrams 111 and 112. This special way of capturing is called capturing en passant, and is abbreviated e.p. En passant is a French expression meaning "in passing." It is as if the Black pawn in Diagram 111 captured the White pawn while it was passing through the b3 square.

En passant capturing is possible only if all the following conditions are satisfied:

1. The pawn doing the capturing must be on the fifth rank, if it is a White pawn, or on the fourth rank, if it is a Black pawn.
2. The pawn doing the capturing and the pawn being captured must be on adjacent files.
3. The pawn to be captured must be on its original square (second rank for White and seventh for Black.)
4. The pawn to be captured must advance two squares in one move (Diagram 111).
5. In reply, the opposite pawn captures the pawn that has advanced two squares as if it had only advanced one square. (Diagrams 109 and 112).

The option to capture en passant must be exercised by the capturing side on its very first move following the two-square advance of the enemy pawn. If a player chooses not to capture en passant, the position will be as shown in Diagram 111. If, in Diagram 111, Black does not capture en passant and makes some other move instead, the White pawn is safe from being captured en passant for the rest of the game.

An en passant capture is compulsory only when it is the only legal move available — e.g., if it is the only move a player has to get his King out of check (see Diagram 113).

113

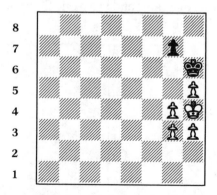

8
7
6
5
4
3
2
1

a b c d e f g h

By the move **1. ... g7-g5** the Black pawn checks the King. Only the rule "en passant" can save the White King.

On the other hand, an en passant capture is of course not permitted if it would expose the player's King to check. For example, in Diagram 114 Black to move can checkmate White with the move 1. ... g7-g5.

114

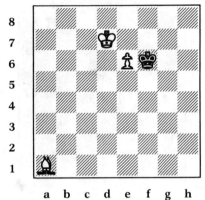

White cannot get out of check by capturing en passant, since to do so would mean exposing his King to check by the Black Rook along the h-file.

Remember that only pawns can capture en passant and that only pawns can be captured en passant.

HOMEWORK
I. Diagrams 115–120
(answers at the end)

115

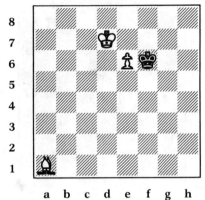

What was White's last move?

_____

_____

_____

116

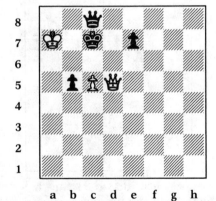

a) White to play and checkmate in one move.
b) What was Black's last move?

_____

_____

_____

In Diagrams 117–120, White is to play and checkmate in one move. Write down your answers in the space provided below.

119

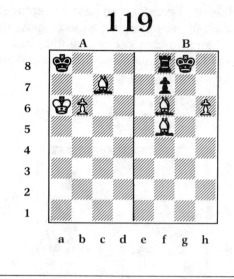

117

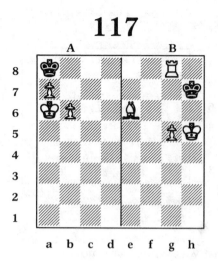

_____

_____

_____

118

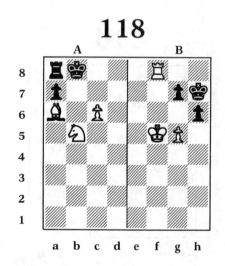

_____

_____

_____

120

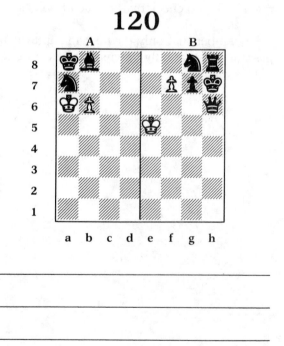

_____

_____

_____

II. Exercises

Write down your answers in the space below.

1. Move the Queen from d1 to g8 via b7 and write down its route.

_____

_____

_____

2. Move the Bishop from c1 to b8 via g7 and write down its route.

_____

_____

_____

3. Without looking at a chessboard name the squares where:
   a) the c1-a3 diagonal crosses the a1-h8 diagonal.
   b) the f1-h3 diagonal crosses the h1-a8 diagonal.

_____

_____

_____

4. Construct:
   a) a position in which a Black pawn could capture en passant **e4xd3** or **e4xf3**, depending on White's previous move.
   b) a position in which either of **two** White pawns could capture a Black pawn en passant.

_____

_____

_____

Homework Answers
I. Diagrams 115–120

D-115 White's last move had to be **1. d5xe6 e.p.** (en passant).

D-116 a) **1. c5xb6 e.p. checkmate**
b) **b7-b5**

D-117 a) **b6-b7 checkmate**
b) **g5-g6 checkmate**

D-118 a) **1.c6-c7 checkmate**
b) **1. g5-g6 checkmate**

D-119 a) **1. b6-b7 checkmate**
b) **1. h6-h7 checkmate**

D-120 a) **1. b6-b7 checkmate**
b) **1. f7-f8N checkmate**

II. Exercises

1. Qd1-d5-b7-b8-g8. This is just one possibility. There are several other four-move routes possible.

2. Bc1-b2 (or h6) **-g7-e5-b8.**

3. a) b2. b) g2.

4. a) White pawn on d4 and f4 and a Black pawn on e4. If White has played **1. d2-d4** on his last move, Black can capture **1. ... e4xd3 e.p.**, while if White has just played **1. f2-f4**, then Black can capture **1. ... e4xf3 e.p.**

b) White pawn on d5 and f5 and a Black pawn which has just played **1. ... e7-e5.** White has a choice between **d5xe6 e.p.** and **f5xe6 e.p.**

43

Lesson Seven

Castling

Check Lesson Six homework if necessary.

Review Questions:
1. What are the ways of getting out of check?
2. What happens if a King cannot get out of check?
3. How many moves does a Knight need to get from a1 to b2? Give an example.
4. How many moves does a Knight need to get from h1 to a8? Give an example.
5. When will a King that is standing beside a pawn not be within capturing distance of the pawn after the pawn moves?
6. Can a Black pawn on d4 capture en passant if a White pawn moves from e2 to e4?
7. A Black pawn is on e4. White moves d2-d4 and then f2-f4, while the Black pawn is still on e4. After White moves f2-f4, which pawn can be captured en passant?
8. Can en passant captures occur near the end of a game, or only near the beginning?

Answers to Review Questions
1. A player can get out of check in any of three ways:
   a) by moving his King to a safe square;
   b) by interposing any of his men between his King and the checking piece;
   c) by capturing the checking piece.
2. When none of the above methods can be applied, the King is checkmated and the game is over — the player whose King has been checkmated loses.
3. A Knight needs four moves to get from a1 to b2; e.g. **Na1-b3-c1-d3-b2.**
4. A Knight needs six moves to get from h1 to a8: e.g. **Nh1-f2-d3-b4-d5-c7-a8.**

5. When the pawn is in its starting position (on the second rank for a White pawn and on the seventh rank for a Black pawn). For example, in Diagram 121 White to move can play **1. h2-h4** and the pawn has escaped from the Black King, and Black to move can play **1. ... b7-b5**, and the Black pawn has escaped from the White King.

121

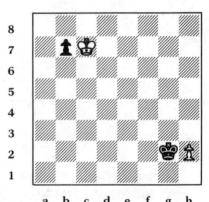

6. Yes.
7. White can capture "en passant" only the f-pawn.
8. The "en passant" rule can be used at any time during a game.

Castling

Castling was introduced into chess in the 14th century. It is an extremely important move. Castling involves moving both the King and the Rook at the same time in a special way, but counts as one move.

Castling helps a player to:

a) provide his King a safe shelter behind his pawns, and

b) bring one of his powerful Rooks into a good position either for attack or for defense.

The King's safety is a prime concern in each game, and it is dangerous to leave it in the middle of the board, where it is more exposed to attack. By castling, a player whisks the King away to the security of the Royal Castle, so to speak!

Castling is optional, but it is a useful move that should not be lightly forsaken. In most games, both the players castle.

Diagram 122 shows that both White and Black can castle either on the Kingside or on the Queenside.

122

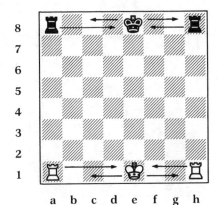

The King moves only two squares in castling, either King's side or Queen's side.

123

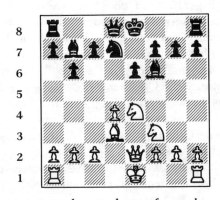

White can castle Queen's side or King's side; Black can castle only King's side.

Diagram 124 shows a position where neither player has castled, and Diagram 125 shows the resulting position after White has castled on the Kingside and Black on the Queenside.

124

125

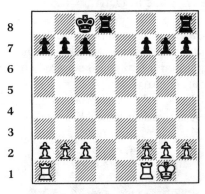

As you can see, in each case, the King moved two squares towards a Rook, and the Rook moved onto the square that the King had crossed. White, when castling on the Kingside, moves his King from e1 to g1 and his Rook from h1 to f1; and when castling on the Queenside moves his King to c1 and his Rook to d1. Black moves his King to g8 and his Rh8 to f8 when castling on the Kingside, and his King to c8 and his Ra8 to d8 when castling on the Queenside.

In chess notation, Kingside castling is written as 0-0, and Queenside castling is written as 0-0-0. Kingside castling is also called castling short, while Queenside castling is also known as castling long.

Castling Rules

A player may castle only once in a game, and only according to the following rules:

1. Castling is not permitted if either the King or the Rook used in castling has already moved at any point in the game. See Diagrams 122, 124 and 125.
2. All the squares between the King and the Rook must be empty. Neither can jump over any other pieces. That is why Black in Diagram 123 cannot castle on the Queenside and White in Diagram 126 cannot castle on the Kingside.
3. The King must not be in check (castling is not allowed for the purpose of getting out of check). That is why Black cannot castle in Diagram 127.
4. The King may not move into check. That is why Black cannot castle on the Queenside in Diagram 126.
5. The square which the King jumps over should not be under attack by any enemy man. That is why Black cannot castle on the Kingside in Diagram 126.

Note: Castling is possible when the Rook is under attack and also, in the case of Queenside castling, when the b1 or b8 square is under attack by an enemy man.

Let us examine Diagram 126.

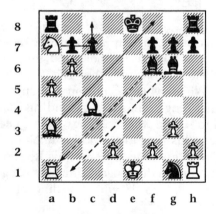

126

Black can't castle.
White can only castle Queenside.

White can only castle on the Queenside. He cannot castle on the Kingside (although he may be able to later) because one of the squares between the King and the King's Rook is occupied by a piece, in this case a Black Knight.

Black cannot castle on either side. He cannot castle on the Queenside (although he may be able to later) because the square on which the King would land, c8, is controlled by an enemy piece, the White Knight on a7. He cannot castle Kingside (although he may be able to later) because in order to do so the King would have to cross a square controlled by an enemy man (the Bishop on a3, or Ba3, attacks the square f8.)

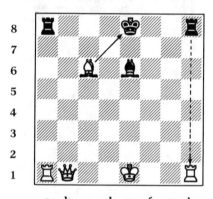

127

Black can't castle.
White can only castle Kingside.

In Diagram 127, Black cannot castle because his King is in check by the White Bishop on c6. If Black gets out of check by capturing the Bishop or interposing a piece on d7, he may be able to castle later on. If he gets out of check by moving his King, he can never castle for the rest of the game (see Rule 1 above). White cannot castle on the Queenside because one of the squares between the King and the Queen's Rook, b1, is occupied by a piece, in this case the White Queen. However, White can castle on the Kingside.

Now you know how to move, capture, and castle. You are ready to play real chess!

HOMEWORK
I. Diagrams 128–133

In Diagrams 128–130, can White castle on either side if it is his turn to move? Can Black to move castle on either side?

130

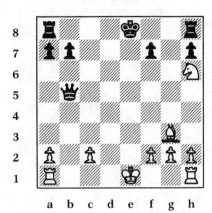

128

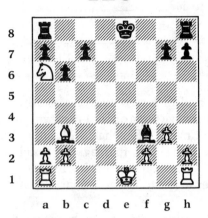

_____

_____

_____

In Diagrams 131–133, it is White's turn to move. (Funny Puzzles).

131

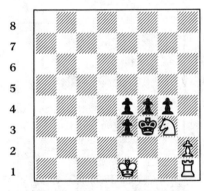

Checkmate in one move.

_____

_____

_____

129

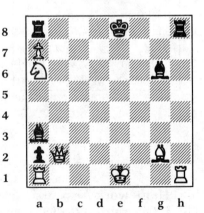

_____

_____

132

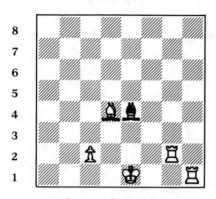

a b c d e f g h

Place the Black King so that White checkmates him in one move. Two solutions.

_____

_____

_____

133

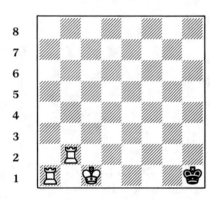

a b c d e f g h

Checkmate in half a move.

_____

_____

_____

II. Exercises

Write down your answers in the spaces provided.

1. How many moves does a Knight on c3 need to get:

    a) to c4? _____

    b) to d4? _____

    c) to c6? _____

    d) to e5? _____

First find all these moves on a board and then try to visualize them on the board without moving the Knight. After that, without looking at the board at all, try to imagine a Knight on c3 and name the squares that it will need to cross in order to get to c4, d4, c6, and e5.

2. Construct a position on the diagram below where the White King and two White Bishops have checkmated the Black King.

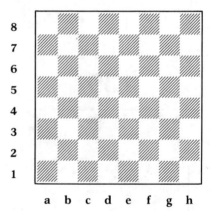

a b c d e f g h

Homework Answers
I. Diagrams 128–133

D-128 White can castle only on the Kingside and Black only on the Queenside.

D-129 Both White and Black can castle on either side.

D-130 Both White and Black can castle only on the Queenside.

D-131 1. 0-0

D-132 The Black King must be place on c1 or

f3, when White can checkmate it by castling on the Kingside (**1. 0-0**).

D-133 White is in the process of castling on the Queenside — he has so far completed half the move by placing his King on c1. By making the other half of the move and shifting the Rook from a1 to d1, White will checkmate Black.

II. Exercises

1. A Knight on c3 needs:
a) 3 moves to reach c4: e.g. **Nc3-e4-d2-c4;**
b) 2 moves to reach d4: e.g. **Nc3-b5-d4;**
c) 3 moves to reach c6: e.g. **Nc3-b5-d4-c6;** and
d) 4 moves to reach e5: e.g. **Nc3-b5-d4-c6-e5.**

2. An example is shown in Diagram 134.

134

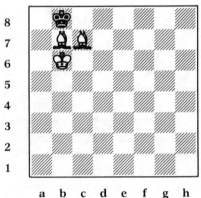

Lesson Eight

Relative Values Of The Chess Forces

Check Lesson Seven homework (if necessary).

Review Questions:
1. What is the name of the move which involves moving a King and a Rook at the same time?
2. Which piece can jump over another one only once in a game?
3. How many moves would a Knight on a1 need to visit all three other corners and then come back to a1?
4. Can a player castle with a Rook if it is under attack?
5. Can a player get his King out of check by castling?
6. Can a player castle if in doing so his King would have to cross a square attacked by an enemy man?
7. Can a player castle if in doing so his Rook has to cross a square attacked by an enemy man, but his King doesn't?
8. Can a player castle if after doing so his King would be in check?

Answers to Review Questions

1. Castling.
2. A Rook — it jumps over the King during castling.
3. A Knight on a1 will need twenty moves to visit the three other corners and then return to a1. For example: 1. Na1-c2 2. Nc2-a3 3. Na3-b5 4. Nb5-c7 5. Nc7-a8 6. Na8-b6 7. Nb6-c8 8. Nc8-e7 9. Ne7-g6 10. Ng6-h8 11. Nh8-f7 12. Nf7-h6 13. Nh6-g4 14. Ng4-f2 15. Nf2-h1 16. Nh1-g3 17. Ng3-f1 18. Nf1-d2 19. Nd2-b3, and 20. Nb3-a1.
4. Yes.
5. No.
6. No.
7. Yes.
8. No.

Relative Values of the Chess Forces

It is very important to know the value of the various men so that in trading men you don't give up a strong one for a weak one. A player who gets an advantage by trading his weaker men for his opponent's stronger ones can use this advantage to force checkmate or to queen a pawn and then force checkmate.

The value of a chessman is determined by its maneuverability and range, by the number of squares it can cross in one move, by the number of squares it can control, by how rapidly and deeply it can infiltrate the enemy positions, and by how dangerous a threat it can pose to the opponent. The experience of many games has shown that the approximate relative values of the chessmen are as follows:

Queen	— 9 points
Rook	— 5 points
Bishop	— 3 points
Knight	— 3 points
Pawn	— 1 point

The King cannot be captured, and so it is not included in the above list. In the center of the board it controls eight squares, while in a corner it is not even half as strong, controlling only three squares (see Diagram 135).

135

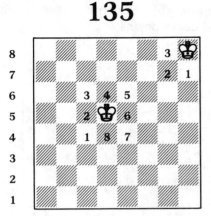

The King differs from the other men, however, in that its value is not determined by its strength. In the opening and the middlegame the King is a weak piece that must be safely guarded. In the endgame, when it is not in danger of being checkmated by the opponent's men, the King gains power considerably, varying in strength between a Bishop (or Knight) and a Rook.

The strongest piece is the Queen. From a central position it controls 27 squares, nearly half the board (Diagram 136).

136

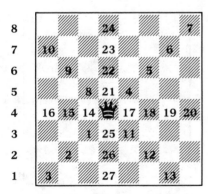

It is weaker in the corner, but still controls 21 squares (Diagram 137).

137

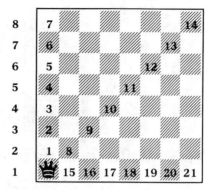

The next strongest is the Rook. No matter where it is on the board, it controls 14 squares (Diagram 138).

138

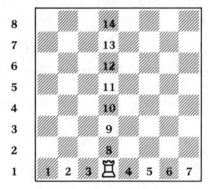

The Bishop controls 13 squares from a central position (Diagram 139) but only seven squares from a corner (Diagram 140).

139

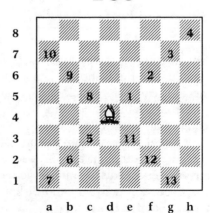

140

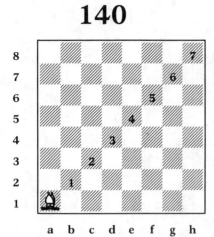

Although it can control almost as many squares as a Rook, the Bishop is much weaker. The reason is that it can move only on squares of one color, and thus cannot threaten enemy pieces on squares of the other color. The Queen, Rook, and Bishop are all long-range pieces, as they can attack hostile pieces at any distance.

The Knight controls eight squares from a central position and only two from a corner (Diagram 141).

141

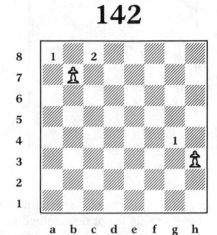

The Knight controls fewer squares than the Bishop, and unlike the Bishop, it is not a long-range piece. It can only attack enemy pieces that are nearby. On the other hand, the Knight has greater maneuverability, being able to jump over other pieces, and it can attack enemy pieces on both light and dark squares. These advantages and disadvantages generally balance out, and so the Knight and Bishop are considered to be of equal value.

Diagram 142 illustrates the attacking capabilities of pawns.

142

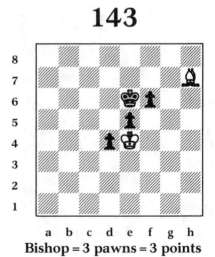

The Rook pawns (a-pawn and h-pawn) control only one square each, while the other pawns all control two squares each. The pawns are the weakest units in the chess army. However, we must not disdain them, since they have the potential of changing into a Queen or any other piece.

Diagrams 143–146 show positions in which the White and Black men are of equal value:

143

Bishop = 3 pawns = 3 points

144

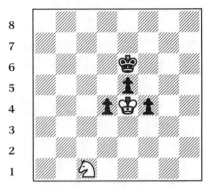

Knight = 3 pawns = 3 points

145

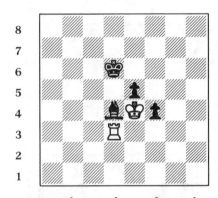

Rook = Bishop + 2 pawns = 5 points

146

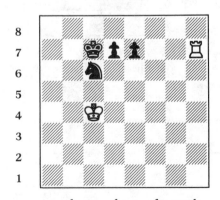

Rook = Knight + 2 pawns = 5 points

Similarly, you can figure out that two Bishops are stronger than a Rook, that a Queen is more valuable than a Rook and a Bishop, and so on.

When playing, you should keep in mind the relative values of the various men, but at the same time never forget that the final goal is to checkmate your opponent's King. It is worth it to sacrifice any number of your pieces if by doing so you can checkmate your opponent's King.

HOMEWORK

In doing the homework, remember that
    Queen = 9 points
    Rook = 5 points
    Bishop = 3 points
    Knight = 3 points
    Pawn = 1 point

From now on, you should keep track of the point count during your games, but never forget that checkmate is of greater value than any number of points.

I. Diagrams 147–154

147

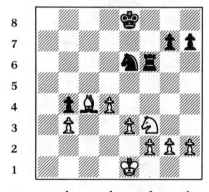

Who has more points — White or Black?

_____

_____

_____

53

148

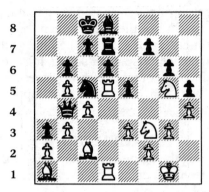

Which position is better and why?

_____

_____

_____

150

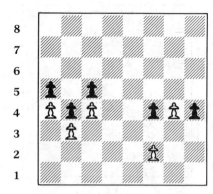

White's last move was **g2-g4**. How many moves has Black in this position?

_____

_____

_____

149

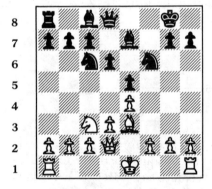

Who has more points — Black or White?

_____

_____

_____

151

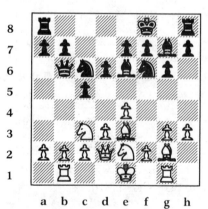

Is castling possible in this position for White and Black?

_____

_____

_____

152

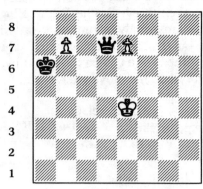

White to play. Can they win?

_____

_____

_____

153

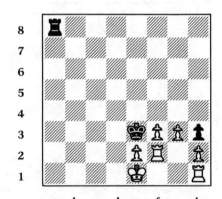

White to play. Can he win?

_____

_____

_____

154

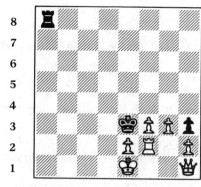

White to move. How will the game end?

_____

_____

_____

II. Exercises

1. Without looking at the board, name the squares that the King crosses in going from e1 to h8 via f5.

_____

_____

_____

2. Move a Rook from a1 in such a way that it lands on every square of the board exactly once and then comes back to a1. (Mark your answer on the diagram below).

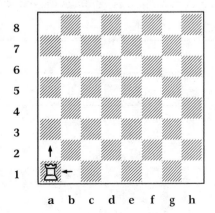

HOMEWORK ANSWERS
I. Diagrams 147–154

D-147 White is one point up and has chances of winning.

D-148 White is two points up and has chances of winning.

D-149 White and Black have each lost six points, and the game is even.

D-150 Black has four moves: 1. ... f4-f3; 1. ... f4xg3 en passant; 1. ... h4xg3 en passant; and 1. ... h4-h3.

D-151 Neither side can castle: White, because his Rooks have already moved, and Black, because his King has already moved.

D-152 Yes. Although Black is seven points up, White wins here thanks to the wonderful ability of pawns to turn into any other piece when they reach the other end of the board: 1. **b7-b8N +** and White captures the Black Queen the next move.

D-153 White can win only if his King and the Rook on h1 have not made any moves at all so far in the game. In that case White can castle and should win, since he is eight points up.

D-154 Black wins although White is a whole 12 points up. Black is threatening checkmate with **1. ... Ra8-a1** and the White Queen and Rook are in such a bad position that they cannot help their King. So the White King can avoid checkmate only by running away with 1. **Ke1-d1**, but then Black replies with **Ra8-a1 +**, capturing the White Queen the next move and the White Rook the move after.

II. Exercises

1. One possibility is: 1. Ke1-e2 2. Ke2-e3 3. Ke3-e4 4. Ke4-f5 5. Kf5-g6 6. Kg6-g7 7. Kg7-h8.

2. See Diagram 155.

155

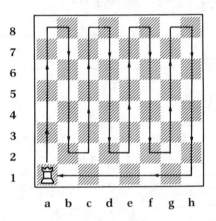

Lesson Nine
How Games Are Drawn

Check Lesson Eight homework if necessary.

Review Questions
What is more valuable:
1. A Knight or a Bishop?
2. A Knight and a pawn, or a Rook?
3. A Queen or two Rooks?
4. A Queen, or two Bishops and a Knight?
5. A Queen, or two Knights and a Bishop?
6. A Knight or four pawns?
7. A Bishop or three pawns?
8. A Rook or two Knights?
9. A Rook, or a Bishop and two pawns?
10. A King or a Queen?

Answers to Review Questions
1. A Bishop and a Knight are each worth three points, so neither is stronger — they are equal in value.
2. A Knight (three points) and a pawn (one point) are worth a total of four points, so they are weaker than a Rook (five points).
3. Since a Rook is worth five points, two Rooks are worth $2 \times 5 = 10$ points, so they are a bit stronger than a Queen (nine points).
4. Two Bishops (three points each for a total of six) and a Knight (three points) are worth a total of nine points and so are equal to a Queen (nine points).
5. Two Knights (three points each for a total of six) and a Bishop (three points) are worth a total of nine points and so are equal to a Queen (nine points).
6. Since a pawn is worth one point, four pawns are worth four points and so are stronger than a Knight, which is worth only three points.
7. Since a pawn is worth one point, three pawns are worth three points and so are equal in strength to a Bishop, which is also worth three points.
8. Since a Knight is worth three points, two Knights are worth six points and so are stronger than a Rook, which is worth only five points.
9. Since a pawn is worth one point, two pawns are worth two points. A Bishop is worth three points. So a Bishop and two pawns together are worth a total of $3 + 2 = 5$ points, and are equal to a Rook, which is also worth five points.
10. The King is of course more valuable than any other chess man.

How Games Are Drawn
Chess games usually end in victory for one player and defeat for the other. In some games, however, neither player is able to checkmate his opponent's King. In such cases, neither player wins, and the game ends in a draw. Here are some ways in which a draw can result: perpetual check, stalemate, or not enough material to force checkmate.

Perpetual Check
Perpetual check is a term which refers to the situation when one player checks the opponent's King endlessly, without, however, being able to checkmate it. Diagrams 156 and 157 show typical cases of perpetual check. It is most often a Queen that gives perpetual check, but the Bishop, Rook, and Knight are also capable of doing so.

Diagram 156 shows perpetual check by the Queen.

156

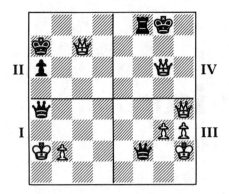

In 156-I, The Black Queen uses d1 and a4 for perpetual check. The only way for White to get out of check in the diagram is to move his King to b1. Then Black moves his Queen to d1 and again checks the White King, which must move back to a2, allowing the Black Queen to check from a4. Black can thus keep checking the White King forever by moving his Queen back and forth between a4 and d1, and so the game is a draw.

In 156-II, the White Queen moves back and forth between c7 and c8. In 156-III, the Black Queen gives perpetual check from f1 and f2, and in 156-IV, the White Queen shuttles back and forth between g6 and h6.

157

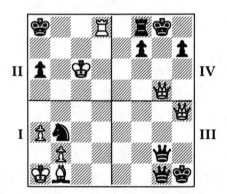

In Diagram 157-I, the Black Knight gives perpetual check to the White King by moving from b3 to c1 and back to b3 (... **Nb3-c1**, ... **Nc1-b3**), since the White King can only move to and fro between a1 and a2.

In 157-II, the White Rook can give perpetual

check from d8 and d7.

In 157-III, Black has an extra Queen. He should have won earlier, but he made a mistake and allowed the position in the diagram to occur. Here White can get a draw by giving perpetual check. No matter which Black Queen interposes, White can always check either on e4, e1 or h4.

In 157-IV, the White Queen can give perpetual check from g5 and f6, forcing the Black King to move back and forth between g8 and h8.

Perpetual check helps players to escape with a draw in games that they would otherwise lose. All players find it useful at some time or another, even World Champions.

Stalemate

A player can find himself in a situation where, although it is his turn to move, and his King is not in check, he has no legal moves. Any move that he made would put his King in check. Such a situation is called stalemate, and the player is said to be stalemated. The difference between stalemate and checkmate is that in stalemate, the King is not in check, while in checkmate, it is in check and cannot get out of it. A stalemate is a drawn game, while a checkmate is a loss for the player whose King is checkmated.

Stalemate occurs only if the player cannot make any legal moves at all. If his King cannot move, but he can move some other piece, he is not stalemated, and must move the other piece, even if it is dangerous to do so and will cause him to lose the game.

Diagrams 158-161 show typical stalemate positions. In all positions in Diagrams 158 and 159, it is White's turn to move. In each case, the King is not in check, but neither does it have any legal moves, since any move would put it in check.

158

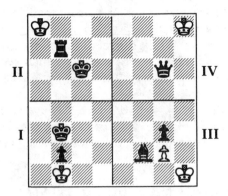

159

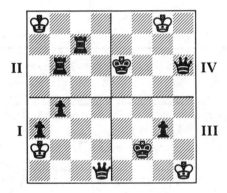

In the eight positions in Diagrams 160 and 161, it is Black's turn to play, but any move would put his King in check. Therefore, the game in each case is a draw by stalemate, since Black's King is not in check and at the same time Black cannot make any legal move on his turn.

160

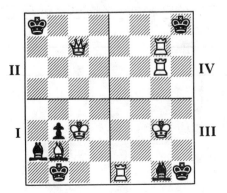

161

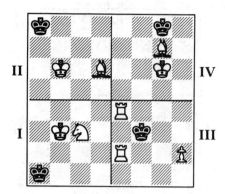

At first, the difference between checkmate and stalemate might not seem very big. In both cases, the King has no moves. But in checkmate, the King is in check, and that is very important. Checkmate wins, but stalemate draws.

Stalemate is often the last chance of a player who is losing. If you happen to have more men than your opponent and you think you can win easily, don't start playing carelessly, or else your opponent might escape with a stalemate. On the other hand, if you are losing, you should try to bring about a stalemate position, since a draw is better than a loss. Stalemate often is the result of a mistake by the player who has the advantage, but sometimes it is the logical end to a game in which both players have played equally well.

It is advisable for beginners to announce "stalemate," "check," or "checkmate" although according to the rules of play it is not compulsory to do so.

Not Enough Material

When neither player has enough material to checkmate, the game is a draw. Thus:

a)   If each player only has a King left, neither can checkmate the opponent.

b)   A King and a Knight alone cannot checkmate a lone King.

c)   A King and a Bishop alone cannot checkmate a lone King.

d)   If each of the players has only a King and a Bishop, and the Bishops are on the same color, then neither side can checkmate the other.

A King and a Knight (or a Bishop) alone can

only stalemate the enemy King, never checkmate it (see Diagram 161-1, II, IV).

HOMEWORK
I. Diagrams 162-169

162

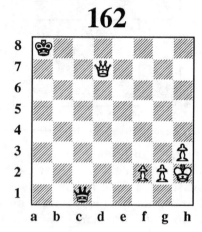

Black to start and make a draw in two ways.

_____

_____

_____

163

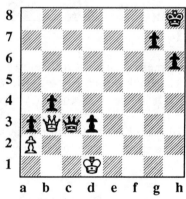

How will the game end if White is to move and if Black is to move?

_____

_____

_____

164

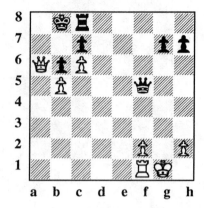

Black to move. Can he draw?

_____

_____

_____

165

White to move and draw.

_____

_____

_____

166

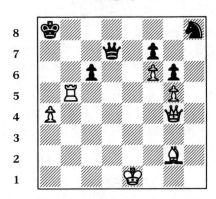

White played **Qg4xd7**. Is it a good move?

_____

_____

_____

168

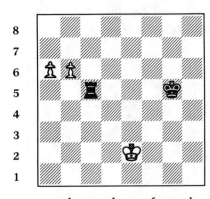

Black to move. Can he stop the White pawns?

_____

_____

_____

167

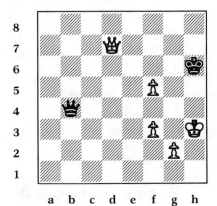

Black to play and draw.

_____

_____

_____

169

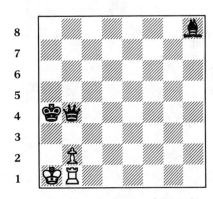

Black to move. Checkmate in one move.

_____

_____

_____

II. Exercises

1. Place five Queens on the diagram below in such a way that together they attack all 64 squares on the board.

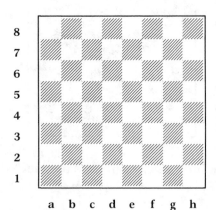

2. Make up a position on the diagram below in which a pawn is not attacked by any enemy men and has a choice of twelve different moves.

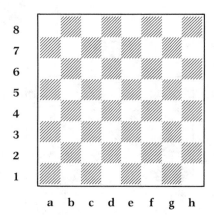

HOMEWORK ANSWERS
I. Diagrams 162-169

D-162 a) **1. ... Qc1-c7 +**. After **2. Qd7xc7** Black is stalemated.

b) **1. ... Qc1-f4 +**. If the White King now retreats to the first rank (**2. Kh1** or **2. Kg1**), then the Black Queen returns to c1 and checks the White King (**2. ... Qc1 +**), giving perpetual check on c1 and f4. If after **1. ... Qc1-f4 +** White does not retreat his King but instead interposes his pawn (**2. g2-g3**), then the Black Queen captures the pawn on f2 (**2. ... Qf4xf2 +**) and gives perpetual check on f2 and f1.

D-163 White to play can draw by giving perpetual check with his Knight by **1. Nf8-g6 + 2. Ng6-f8 +**, etc. Black to play can checkmate White by **1. ... Qf2-h2#**.

D-164 Black to play draws with **1. ... Qf5-g4 +** and after **2. Kh1** the Black Queen gives perpetual check on f3 and g4.

D-165 After **1. Qb3-g8 +**, Black must capture the Queen by **1. ... Kh8xg8**, and White is stalemated.

D-166 **1. Qg4xd7** is a bad move since it stalemates Black. Instead White should have first played **1. Rb5-a5 +** and then captured the Queen on the next move, when Black wouldn't be stalemated any more.

D-167 Black draws by **1. ... Qb4-h4 +**, forcing White to capture the Queen by **52. Kxh4**, after which Black is stalemated.

D-168 No. The Rook cannot hold back both White pawns and one of them will become a Queen.

D-169 **1. ... Qb4-a3#** checkmates White! White cannot capture the Black Queen with his pawn because that would expose his King to check by the Black Bishop on h8.

II. Exercises

1. There are some 4,000 ways of placing five Queens on a chessboard in such a way that together they attack all 64 squares on the board. One way is shown in Diagram 170.

170

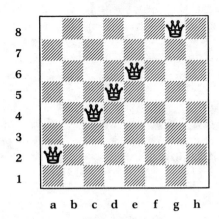

2.   In Diagram 171 the White pawn is not attacked and has a choice of twelve different moves: (1) **1. e7xd8Q**; (2) **1. e7xd8R**; (3) **1. e7xd8B**; (4) **1. e7xd8N**; (5) **1. e7-e8Q**; (6) **1. e7-e8R**; (7) **1. e7-e8B**; (8) **1. e7-e8N**; (9) **1. e7xf8Q**; (10) **1. e7xf8R**; (11) **1. e7xf8B**; and (12) **1. e7xf8N**.

171

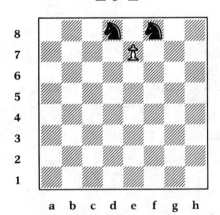

Lesson Ten

How To Record Moves

Check Lesson Nine homework (if necessary)

Review Questions:
1. What is the difference between a checkmate and a stalemate?
2. Make up a stalemate position.
3. Is it possible to win with only a King and a Knight against a lone King?
4. Is it possible to win with only a King and a Bishop against a lone King?
5. White has a King and a Queen, and Black has only his King. Using these pieces only, make up a position in which Black is stalemated.
6. What is perpetual check?
7. Make up a position in which a pawn on e2 has a choice of four different moves.
8. Is it possible for a position to occur in which there are Black pawns on a2, a3, a4, a5, and a6?

Answers to Review Questions

1. In checkmate one of the Kings is in check and cannot get out of it, while in stalemate neither King is in check.
2. An example is shown in Diagram 172, where Black to move is stalemated.

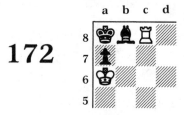

172

3. No.
4. No.
5. An example is shown in Diagram 173, where Black to move is stalemated.

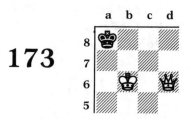

173

6. Perpetual check is a series of endless checks from which the King cannot escape.
7. An example is shown in Diagram 174, where the White pawn on e2 has the choice of moving **1. e2-e3**, **1. e2-e4**, **1. e2xd3**, or **1. e2xf3**.

174

8. Yes. The a6 pawn can get there by advancing from a7 without any captures; the a5 pawn can get there from b6 by capturing (**... b6xa5**); the a4 pawn can get there from c6 by making two captures (**... c6xb5**, and **... b5xa4**); the a3 pawn can get there from d6 by making three captures (**... d6xc5**, **... c5xb4**, and **... b4xa3**);

and the a2 pawn can get there from e6 by making four captures (... e6xd5, ... d5xc4, ... c4xb3, and ... b3xa2). Thus a total of ten enemy men must be captured. This is possible since each side has fifteen men that may be captured during play.

How To Record Moves

In this lesson we will review what we have learned about chess notation. As you know, chess notation is a special kind of language in which each square and man has a name, so that we can record positions and moves. The notation taught in this book is the international algebraic notation.

Once you have mastered the notation system, you will be able to read chess books. Using this system, strong players can even play chess blindfolded.

Algebraic notation is based on a grid system. Each file is designated by a letter, and each rank by a number. Thus, each square is uniquely identified by a symbol consisting of a letter followed by a number.

The files are designated by the letters from a to h, starting from White's left, while the ranks are numbered from 1 to 8, starting from the rank nearest White.

To record a move, you first write down the symbol of the piece that is being moved, then its square of departure, then a hyphen (-), and then the square to which the piece is being moved. If the move is a capture, use an "x" instead of a hyphen. If the move is made by a pawn, its symbol is left out, and only the square of departure, an "x" or a hyphen, and the square of arrival are indicated. For example, **e2-e4** means that the pawn on e2 is moved to e4. Here are some other examples: **Rd1xd6** means that a Rook on d1 captured a man on d6; **a7xb8Q** means that a pawn on a7 captured a piece on b8 and became a Queen; **e7xd8N +** means that a pawn on e7 captured a piece on d8, became a Knight, and gave check to the Black King.

The moves in a game are recorded in two vertical columns, the first for White's moves and the second for Black's moves. Before each of White's moves, there is a number. This number indicates how many moves have been made. Here is an example showing the first five moves in a game:

1. e2-e4	e7-e5
2. Ng1-f3	Nb8-c6
3. Bf1-c4	Ng8-f6
4. d2-d3	Bf8-e7
5. 0-0	0-0

The position after these moves is shown below in Diagram 175.

175

If you want to refer to Black's move by itself, you put three dots before his move. Thus, if we wanted to refer to Black's second move in the above example, we would write **2. ... Nb8-c6**.

Here is another example:

Qd1-h5# means that the White Queen moves from d1 to h5 and checkmates the Black King.

Chess players often record not only games but also positions. In recording a position, first the positions of White's King, Queen, Rooks, Bishops, Knights, and pawns are given, in that order, and then the positions of the Black men, in the same order.

For example, let us record a position from the homework (Diagram 177):

White: Kg1, Qg2, Re8, P's a5, b4, c3
Black: Kh8, Qg6, Nf8, P's a6, b5, c4.
White to move.

The main symbols used in chess notation are as follows: K for King, Q for Queen, B for

Bishop, N for Knight, p for pawn, - for "moves to," x for "captures on," + for "check," # for "checkmate," 0-0 for "castles on the Kingside," 0-0-0 for "castles on the Queenside," ? for bad move, ! for good move, and ... for "Black's move."

The recording of games is obligatory in tournaments and matches. Beginners are advised to start recording their games so that they can later analyze them to try to discover their own and their opponents' mistakes.

HOMEWORK
I. Diagrams 176-181

Write down your answers in the spaces provided.

176

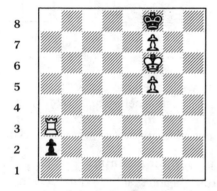

Find and record how on its move:
a)   White wins
b)   Black draws

_____

_____

_____

177

White played **1. Qg2xg6.** Is it a good move?

_____

_____

_____

178

How can Black, on his move, checkmate in one move, and how can he stalemate the White King?

_____

_____

_____

179

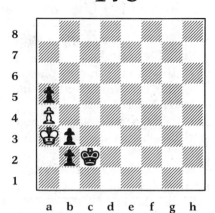

a b c d e f g h

Black to move and checkmate in one move. Find four ways of stalemating the White King.

_____

_____

_____

180

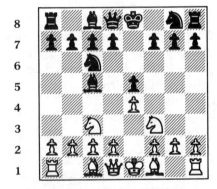

a b c d e f g h

Record three moves by White and Black which have been made in this game.

	WHITE	BLACK
1.		
2.		
3.		

181

Record the position of White and Black pieces after the moves:

1. e2-e4	e7-e5
2. Ng1-f3	Nb8-c6
3. Bf1-c4	Ng8-f6

_____

_____

_____

II. Exercises

Write down your answers in the spaces below.

1. How many Knights of the same color can be placed on a board in such a way that none of them defends another?

_____

_____

2. Is it possible for a position to occur with White pawns on g2, h2, and h3? If not, why not? If so, how?

_____

_____

_____

3. Is it possible for a position to occur with Black pawns on a2, a3, and a4? If so, how? If not, why not?

_____

_____

_____

4. Place five Knights on an empty board in such a way that one of them attacks only two squares, another attacks only three squares, a third attacks only four squares, a fourth attacks only six squares, and the fifth attacks eight squares, with none of the Knights attacking any of the same squares as any other Knight.

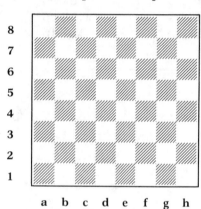

Homework Answers
I. Diagrams 176–181

D-176 a) White to move can checkmate Black with **1. Ra3-a8#.**

       b) Black to move plays **1. ... a2-a1Q +** , and after White captures the Queen with **2. Ra3xa1**, Black is stalemated.

D-177 **1. Qg2xg6** was a very bad move as it stalemated Black. Instead, White could have won by playing **1. Re8xf8 +** .

D-178 Black can checkmate White by **1. ... Bd7-h3#**, and stalemate him by **1. ... Bd7-b5.**

D-179 Black checkmates White by **1. ... b2-b1N#. 1. ... Kc2-c3, 1. ... b2-b1Q, 1. ... b2-b1R,** and **1. ... b2-b1B** all stalemate White.

D-180 This position can be reached after the following moves:

1. e2-e4	**e7-e5**
2. Ng1-f3	**Nb8-c6**
3. Nb1-c3	**Bf8-c5**

D-181 White: Ke1, Qd1, Ra1, Rh1, Bc1, Bc4, Nb1, Nf3, P's a2, b2, c2, d2, e4, f2, g2, h2.

       Black: Ke8, Qd8, Ra8, Rh8, Bc8, Bf8, Nc6, Nf6, P's a7, b7, c7, d7, e5, f7, g7, h7.

II. Exercises

1. Thirty-two, placed on all the light squares or on all the dark squares of the board. This is easy to understand if you remember that a Knight always moves from a light square to a dark square or vice-versa.

2. Such a position (see Diagram 182) is impossible, because a pawn can get to h3 only by moving up from h2 or by capturing from g2.

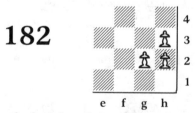

182

Since both the h2 and the g2 pawns are still in their original positions, there is nowhere for the pawn on h3 to have come from.

3. Yes. The pawn on a4 could move up there from a7, while the other two pawns could get where they are by capturing a total of three times: once (**... b4xa3**) for the pawn on a3 and twice (**... c4xb3** and **b3xa2**) for the pawn on a2.

4. See Diagram 183.

183

Knight 1 (on a1) attacks two squares (b3 and c2);

Knight 2 (on g1) attacks three squares (e2, f3, and h3);

Knight 3 (on d8) attacks four squares (b7, c6, e6, and f7);

Knight 4 (on b6) attacks six squares (a4, a8, c4, c8, d5, and d7);

Knight 5 (on e4) attacks eight squares (c3, c5, d2, d6, f2, f6, g3, and g5);

and none of them attacks any squares attacked by any of the other Knights!

Note that the closer a Knight is to the center, the stronger it becomes.

Lesson Eleven
How To Open a Chess Game

Check Lesson Ten homework if necessary.

Review Questions
1. How many squares are there on a chessboard?
2. What are the different kinds of lines formed by squares on a chessboard?
3. What is meant by the "center" of the chessboard?
4. How many Queens can a player have during a game?

Answer Questions 5–8 without looking at a board.
5. Is e7 a light square or a dark one?
6. Name the squares on which the various Black pieces stand at the start of a game.
7. Name the squares that make up the a1-h8 diagonal. Are they light squares or dark ones?
8. At what square does the b-file cross the fourth rank?

Answers to Review Questions
1. Sixty-four.
2. A chessboard contains eight ranks (1 to 8) and eight files (a to h) and many diagonals.
3. The "center" consists of the four squares d4, d5, e4, and e5.
4. A player can have as many as nine Queens, if in addition to keeping his original one he manages to queen all eight of his pawns.
5. The e7 square is a dark square.
6. Ke8, Qd8, Ra8, Rh8, Bc8, Bf8, Nb8 and Ng8.
7. The a1-h8 diagonal is a dark-square diagonal consisting of the squares a1, b2, c3, d4, e5, f6, g7, and h8.
8. Obviously b4!

How to Start a Chess Game
You are now acquainted with the main rules of play. In order to master them better, you need to practise, preferably one hour a day. You can practise against anyone who knows how to play chess, even a computer. Set up the pieces in their starting positions, and away you go!

There are a large number of possibilities for your first move: 16 pawn moves and 4 Knight moves. However, not all of these moves are equally good. Let us look at some examples.

Opening move for White: **1. e2-e4** or **1. d2-d4.**

Opening move for Black: **1. ... e7-e5** or **1. ... d7-d5.** (Diagrams 184 and 185).

184

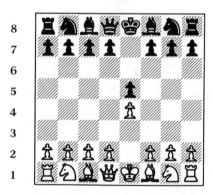

1. e2-e4 (White) 1. ... e7-e5 (Black)
These are good moves to start a game.

185

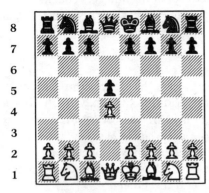

1. d2-d4 (White) 1. ... d7-d5 (Black)
These are good moves to start a game.

These are reasonable moves. Lines are opened up for a Bishop and the Queen.

Opening move for White: **1. g2-g4** or **1. h2-h4**

Opening move for Black: **1. ... g7-g5** or **1. ... h7-h5** (Diagrams 186 and 187).

186

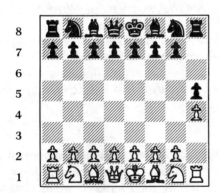

1. h2-h4 (White) 1. ... h7-h5 (Black)
Bad moves. Don't start a game this way.

187

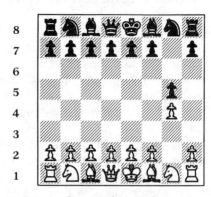

1. g2-g4 (White) 1. ... g7-g5 (Black)
Bad moves. Don't start a game this way.

These moves are not only useless, but also harmful, since the King's position after castling on the Kingside will be exposed, and the opponent will find it easier to checkmate the King.

What are the best ways to start a game? Which pawns should be moved? You have already learned, in Lesson Five, that the center includes the squares d4, d5, e4, and e5. Pieces in the center can easily be transferred to any point on the board, either on the Queenside or on the Kingside. In addition, pieces gain in strength and range when they are in or near the center. For example, a Knight has only two moves if it is in a corner, but eight moves if it is in the center.

In general, a player should aim to achieve the following goals in the opening:

1. the quick development (mobilization) of his pieces;
2. the transfer of his pieces towards the center;
and
3. the safety of his King.
Only thus can a player hope to win.

The experience of the best chessplayers in the world over many centuries has shown that it is wise to adhere to the following principles during the opening stages of a chess game:
1. Always keep in mind the relative strength of each piece. Since the Queen is the strongest one, don't bring it out hastily, or else your opponent will attack it with his Knights, Bishops,

or pawns, thereby forcing your Queen to retreat and furthering his development at your expense.

2. Don't make passive waiting moves such as **a2-a3, a7-a6, h2-h3** or **h7-h6.** Each move should either develop a piece or increase the piece's mobility by opening up files, ranks, or diagonals for them.

3. Try to set up a strong pawn center (e.g. pawns on e4 and d4).

4. Don't waste time by moving one and the same piece repeatedly, at the expense of developing the other pieces.

5. Bring out your Kingside Knight and Bishop, thereby getting ready to transfer your King to a safe place by castling on the Kingside, a move which at the same time develops the King's Rook. After castling, develop your Queenside pieces.

6. Don't attack prematurely. First develop your pieces and castle.

The following is an example of correct opening play by both White and Black:

White	Black
1. e2-e4	e7-e5
2. Ng1-f3	Nb8-c6
3. Bf1-c4	Bf8-c5
4. 0-0	Ng8-f6
5. Nb1-c3	0-0
6. d2-d3	d7-d6

The resultant position is shown in Diagram 188.

188

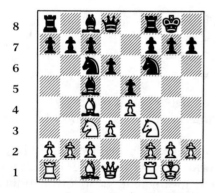

        a   b   c   d   e   f   g   h

Both sides have achieved a good position in the opening and the outcome of the game will depend on who conducts the rest of the game better.

Now let's look at a game where White blunders in the opening and gets checkmated on the second move. This is the shortest game of chess possible, and it's called the "Fool's Mate."

White: 1. f2-f3?

A bad move that leaves the King open to attack. In addition, the pawn on f3 robs the Knight on g1 of its best square.

Black: 1. ... e7-e5

An excellent move, occupying the central square e5 and opening up a diagonal for the f8 Bishop and the Queen.

White: 2. g2-g4??

A terrible move! White completely opens up the way to his King instead of bringing out his pieces.

Black: 2. .,.. Qd8-h4#

Just desserts!

Black had planned to develop his center pawns and then his Knights and Bishops, but after such a terrible move by White, he at once made the most of his opportunity. This example shows you that it is not safe to move your f and g pawns unless you know exactly what you are doing. When your opponent makes such weak moves, try to checkmate him or attack him vigorously.

If your opponent's mistake leads to a situation where you think it is suitable to move your Queen out even in the opening, do so with care, remembering that it is an extremely valuable piece.

The Fool's Mate position is shown in Diagram 189. In this diagram the men have been represented by their letter symbols instead of by their picture symbols. The letters indicating Black men have been circled. Chess players sometimes use this method when solving a problem since it is easy to use; all a person needs is a blank diagram and he can show any position on it. It is advisable to use a pencil, since that way any mistakes can be easily rubbed out and corrected. You will use this method in Chapter Twelv e, the test. There are 20 tests altogether and each student will pick one at random and answer all six questions on it. The test will show how well you have learned the material in the course.

189

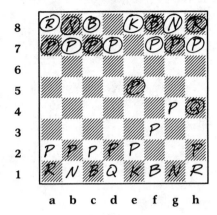

HOMEWORK

1. Review the homework of previous lessons.
2. Teach your parents how to play chess (if they don't know already).
3. Play often, but not more than one hour a day.

You have now finished Level I, **The Rules of Play.**

Lesson Twelve

Test One

1. Where does the a3-f8 diagonal cross the d-file?

---

2. Construct a checkmate position where White has a Queen, Rook, and a King, and Black has only a King.
3. Place a White Queen, two Black Rooks, and the Black King on the board in such a way that Black is checkmated.
4. Place the White King, a White Bishop, the Black King, a Black Bishop, and a Black pawn on the board in such a way that Black is stalemated.
5. Place four White Queens on a quarter-board in such a way that none of them is defended. You can use pawns to represent Queens.
6. Diagram 190. White to move. There is a mistake in the position. Find out what it is and correct it by any means. Once you have done so, White should be able to checkmate Black in one move.

190

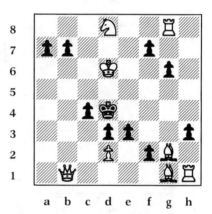

To show different positions on the blank diagrams below, use the following symbols:

WHITE: King— K ; Queen— Q ; Rook— R ; Bishop— B ; Knight— N ; Pawn— P

BLACK: King— Ⓚ ; Queen— Ⓠ ; Rook— Ⓡ ; Bishop— Ⓑ ; Knight— Ⓝ ; Pawn— Ⓟ

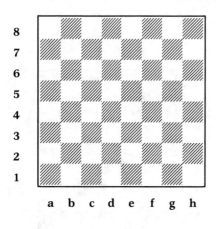

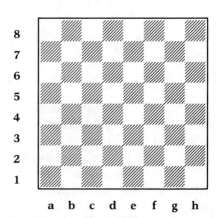

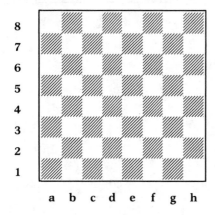

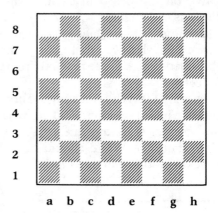

Test Two

1. Where does the b8-h2 diagonal cross the 4th rank?

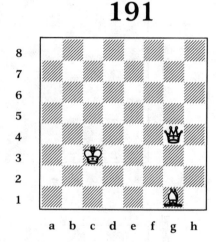

191

2. Construct a checkmate position using the White Queen, the White King, and the Black King.

3. Construct a checkmate positon using two White pawns, a White Bishop, and the Black King.

4. Using any men you want, make up a position where White can checkmate Black by playing pawn takes pawn en passant.

5. Place two White Rooks and two White Bishops on a quarter-board in such a way that none of them is defended by another.

6. Where must the Black King be placed in Diagram 191 so that

    a) Black is checkmated?

    b) Black is stalemated?

    c) White to play can checkmate Black in one move?

To show different positions on the blank diagrams below, use the following symbols:

WHITE: King— K ; Queen— Q ; Rook— R ; Bishop— B ; Knight— N ; Pawn— P
BLACK: King— Ⓚ ; Queen— Ⓠ ; Rook— Ⓡ ; Bishop— Ⓑ ; Knight— Ⓝ ; Pawn— Ⓟ

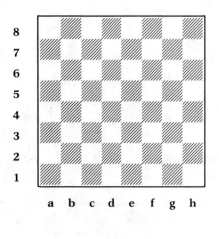

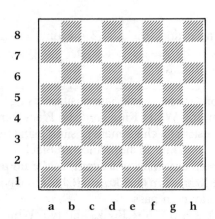

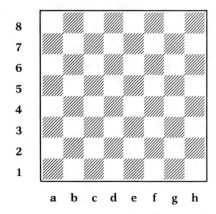

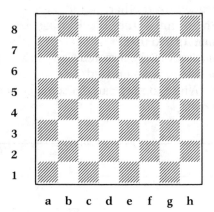

Test Three

1. What is the most number of Queens that a player can have?

---

2. Construct a checkmate position where White has two Rooks and his King and Black has just his King.

3. Construct a position where a White Rook and a White Knight have checkmated Black's King.

4. Find a position in which White can checkmate the Black King in half a move.

5. Place a White King, White Queen, White Rook and White Bishop on a quarter-board in such a way that none of them is defended by another.

6. Diagram 192. In a real chess game, each side can only have one King. But here is a crazy position in which Black has ten Kings! Find a move for White which checkmates all the Black Kings at the same time.

192

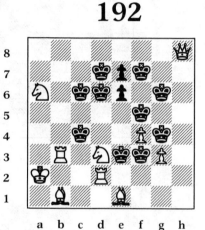

To show different positions on the blank diagrams below use the following symbols:

WHITE: King— K ; Queen— Q ; Rook— R ; Bishop— B ; Knight— N ; Pawn— P
BLACK: King— (K); Queen— (Q); Rook— (R); Bishop— (B); Knight— (N); Pawn—(P)

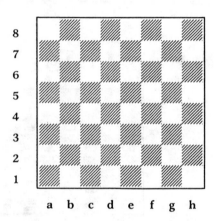

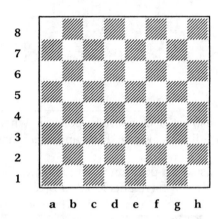

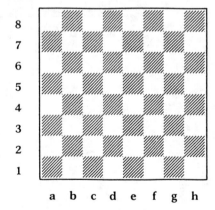

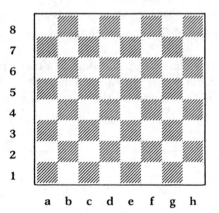

Test Four

1. What is the most number of Rooks that one player can have?

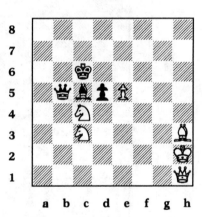

193

2. Construct a position where White, with his King, a Rook, and a Bishop, has checkmated Black's King.

3. Place a Black King, Black pawn, White King, and White Knight on the board in such a way that Black is checkmated.

4. Construct a position in which a pawn has a choice of twelve different moves without itself being under attack any any time, either before or after moving.

5. White has two Rooks, a light-square bishop, and a dark-square Bishop. Place them all on a quarter-board in such a way that each piece defends and is defended by exactly one other piece.

6. Diagram 193. A tricky puzzle! White to checkmate Black in one move.

To show different positions on the blank diagrams below use the following symbols:

WHITE: King— K ; Queen— Q ; Rook— R ; Bishop— B ; Knight— N ; Pawn— P

BLACK: King— Ⓚ; Queen— Ⓠ; Rook— Ⓡ; Bishop— Ⓑ; Knight— Ⓝ; Pawn—Ⓟ

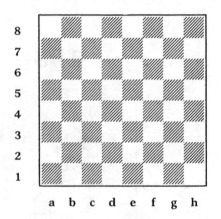

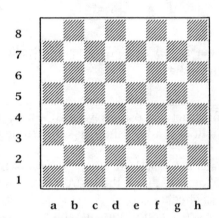

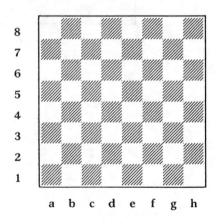

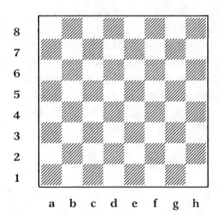

Test Five

1. What is the most number of Bishops that a player can have?

---

2. Construct a checkmate position in which White has a King, Rook, and a Knight, and Black has a lone King.

3. Place a Black King and a White Queen on the board in such a way that Black is stalemated.

4. Set up a position where White and Black each have a King and a Knight, and Black has been checkmated.

5. Place a White King, White Queen, White Bishop, and White Knight on a quarter-board in such a way that none of them is defended by another.

6. Diagram 194. Can either player, if it is his turn to move, avoid checkmating the other?

194

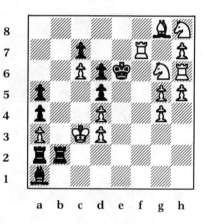

To show different positions on the blank diagrams below use the following symbols:

WHITE: King— K ; Queen— Q ; Rook— R ; Bishop— B ; Knight— N ; Pawn— P

BLACK: King—Ⓚ; Queen—Ⓠ; Rook—Ⓡ; Bishop—Ⓑ; Knight—Ⓝ; Pawn—Ⓟ

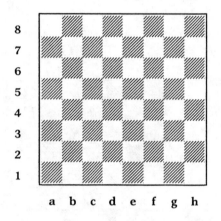

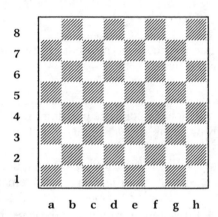

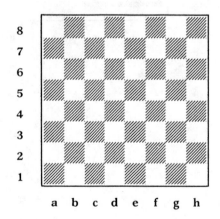

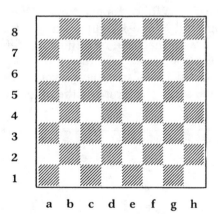

Test Six

1. What is the most number of Knights that one player can have?

2. Construct a position in which White, with a King and Rook, has checkmated Black's lone King.
3. Place two White Rooks and a Black King on a board in such a way that Black is stalemated.
4. Construct a position in which White, with two Bishops and a King, has checkmated Black's lone King.
5. Place a White King, Queen, Rook, and Knight on a quarter-board in such a way that none of them is defended by another.
6. Diagram 195. White to play and checkmate Black in one move.

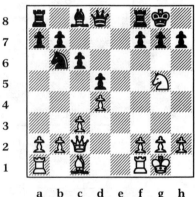

To show different positions on the blank diagrams below, use the following symbols:

WHITE: King— K ; Queen— Q ; Rook— R ; Bishop— B ; Knight— N ; Pawn— P
BLACK: King— Ⓚ ; Queen— Ⓠ ; Rook— Ⓡ ; Bishop— Ⓑ ; Knight— Ⓝ ; Pawn— Ⓟ

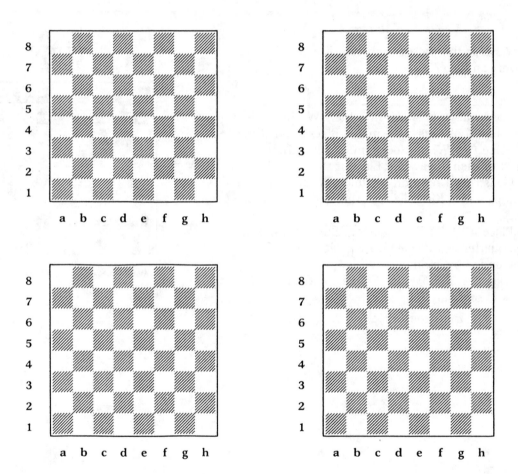

Test Seven

1. Can a pawn remain a pawn when it reaches the last rank, or does it have to turn into a piece?

2. Construct a position where White, with a Bishop, Knight, and King, has checkmated a lone Black King.

3. Place a Black King, White Rook, and White Knight on a board in such a way that Black is stalemated.

4. Place a White King, White Bishop, and White Knight on a board in such a way that the Knight has no moves.

5. Place a White Queen, White Rook, White Bishop, and White Knight on a quarter-board in such a way that none of them is defended by another.

6. Diagram 196. White to play and checkmate Black in one move.

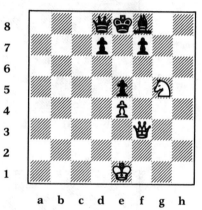

To show different positions on the blank diagrams below, use the following symbols:

WHITE: King— K ; Queen— Q ; Rook— R ; Bishop— B ; Knight— N ; Pawn— P

BLACK: King— Ⓚ ; Queen— Ⓠ ; Rook— Ⓡ ; Bishop— Ⓑ ; Knight— Ⓝ ; Pawn— Ⓟ

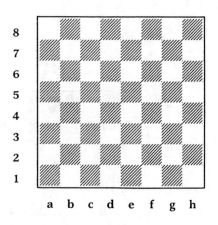

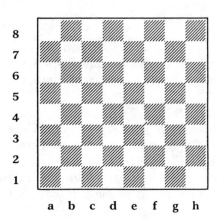

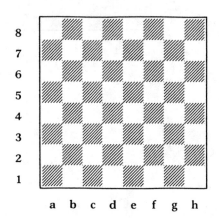

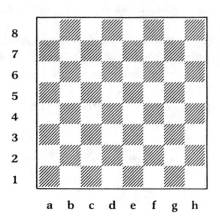

Test Eight

1. When a pawn reaches the last rank, can it turn into a King?

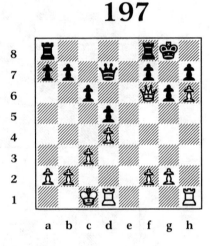

197

2. Construct a position in which White, with his King and two Knights, has checkmated a lone Black King.

3. Place a Black King, White Rook, and White pawn on a board in such a way that Black is stalemated.

4. White and Black each have a King, Queen, Bishop and Rook. Place all the eight men on a quarter-board in such a way that none of them is attacked by an enemy man.

5. Place a White King, White Rook, White Bishop, and White Knight on a quarter-board in such a way that none of them is defended by another.

6. Diagram 197. White to play and checkmate Black in one move.

To show different positions on the blank diagrams below use the following symbols:

WHITE: King— K ; Queen— Q ; Rook— R ; Bishop— B ; Knight— N ; Pawn— P
BLACK: King— (K) ; Queen— (Q) ; Rook— (R) ; Bishop— (B) ; Knight— (N) ; Pawn— (P)

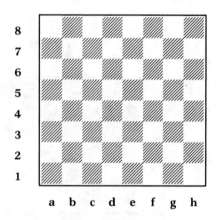

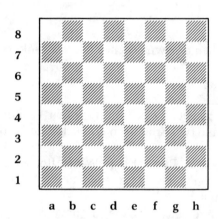

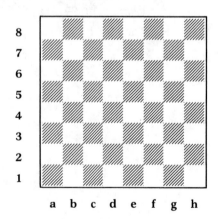

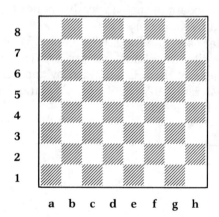

Test Nine

1. Is castling possible when a Rook is under attack?

2. Place a Black King, Black Bishop, White King and White Bishop on a board in such a way that Black is checkmated. White's is a dark-square Bishop, and Black's is a light-square one.

3. Place a Black King, White King, and White Rook on a board in such a way that Black has been stalemated.

4. Place eight pawns (four of each color) on the board in such a way that each player has a choice of six different captures.

5. Can White castle if he has his King on d1 and a Rook on a1?

6. Diagram 198. White to play and checkmate Black in one move.

198

To show different positions on the blank diagrams below, use the following symbols:

WHITE: King— K ; Queen— Q ; Rook— R ; Bishop— B ; Knight— N ; Pawn— P
BLACK: King— Ⓚ ; Queen— Ⓠ ; Rook— Ⓡ ; Bishop— Ⓑ ; Knight— Ⓝ ; Pawn— Ⓟ

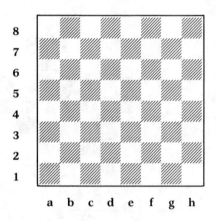

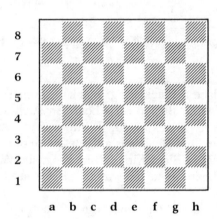

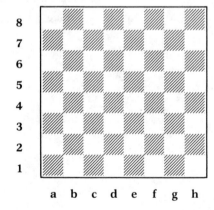

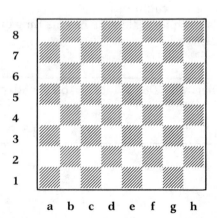

Test Ten

1. Can a player castle if that would involve moving his Rook across a square attacked by an enemy piece, but his King would not have to cross or land on a square attacked by an enemy piece?

---

2. Construct a position where White, with his King and two Pawns, has checkmated a lone Black King.

3. Place a Black King, Black Knight, White King and White pawn on a board in such a way that the White pawn has four ways of checkmating Black in one move by being promoted into a Rook or a Queen.

4. Place the eight Black pieces along with the White King on a quarter-board in such a way that White is not in check and has a choice of three captures.

5. Using a White King, a White Bishop, two White pawns, and a Black King, make up a position in which one of the White pawns can checkmate Black by being promoted into a Bishop.

6. Diagram 199. White to play and checkmate Black in one move.

199

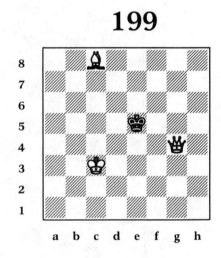

To show different positions on the blank diagrams below, use the following symbols:

WHITE: King— K ; Queen— Q ; Rook— R ; Bishop— B ; Knight— N ; Pawn— P

BLACK: King— Ⓚ; Queen— Ⓠ; Rook— Ⓡ; Bishop— Ⓑ; Knight— Ⓝ; Pawn— Ⓟ

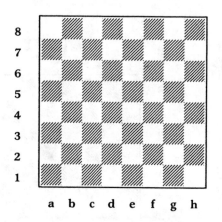

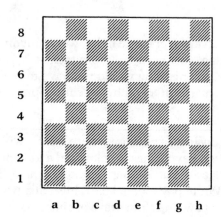

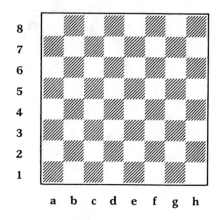

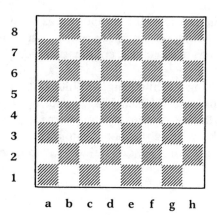

Test Eleven

1. If White has moved his pawn from c2 to c3, and later, on another move, from c3 to c4, can the pawn be captured en passant by a Black pawn on d4?

---

2. Place a Black King, Black Knight, White King, and White Bishop on a board in such a way that Black has been checkmated.

3. Place a Black King, White King, and White Knight on a board in such a way that Black has been stalemated.

4. Place eight pawns (four of each color) on a board in such a way that none of them can move or capture.

5. Can White castle if he has his King on e1 and a Rook on h1, while Black has a Bishop on g3 and there is no man on f2? _____

6. Diagram 200. White to play and checkmate Black in one move.

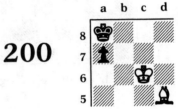

200

To show different positions on the blank diagrams below, use the following symbols:

WHITE: King— K ; Queen— Q ; Rook— R ; Bishop— B ; Knight— N ; Pawn— P

BLACK: King— Ⓚ; Queen— Ⓠ; Rook— Ⓡ; Bishop— Ⓑ; Knight— Ⓝ; Pawn— Ⓟ

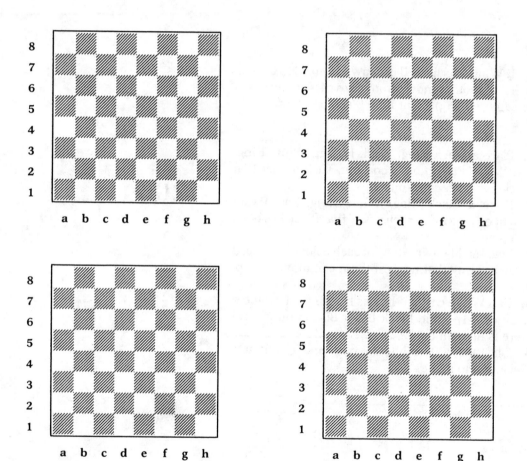

Test Twelve

1. What is the difference between a checkmate and a stalemate?

2. Construct a position in which White, with a King, Bishop, and pawn, has checkmated Black's lone King

3. Place a Black King, White King, and White Bishop on a board in such a way that Black is stalemated.

4. Arrange the two Kings along with a White Queen, White Rook, White Bishop, and White Knight on a quarter-board in such a way that each of the four White pieces can checkmate Black in one move.

5. Place a White Rook, White Bishop, Black King, Black Rook, Black Bishop, and two Black pawns on a board in such a way that the White Bishop can give perpetual check.

6. Diagram 201. White to play and checkmate Black in one move.

201

To show different positions on the blank diagrams below, use the following symbols:

WHITE: King— K ; Queen— Q ; Rook— R ; Bishop— B ; Knight— N ; Pawn— P
BLACK: King— Ⓚ; Queen— Ⓠ; Rook— Ⓡ; Bishop— Ⓑ; Knight— Ⓝ; Pawn— Ⓟ

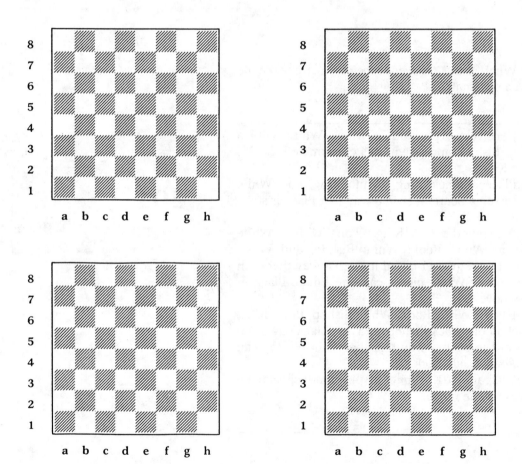

Test Thirteen

1. There is a Black pawn on e4. White first moves d2-d4, and later f2-f4. Which pawn can Black capture en passant after White's move f2-f4?

2. Place a Black King, Black Bishop, White King, and White Knight on a board in such a way that Black is checkmated.

3. Place a Black King, Black pawn, and White Queen on a board in such a way that White can give perpetual check to the Black King.

4. Set up a stalemate position using a White King, White pawn, and two Black Rooks without putting any men on any of the board's edges.

5. Diagram 202—I. White to play and checkmate black in one move.

6. Diagram 202—II. White to play and checkmate Black in one move. This is a tricky puzzle!

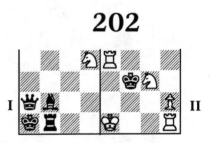

202

I   II

To show different positions on the blank diagrams below, use the following symbols:

WHITE: King— K ; Queen— Q ; Rook— R ; Bishop— B ; Knight— N ; Pawn— P
BLACK: King— Ⓚ; Queen— Ⓠ; Rook— Ⓡ; Bishop— Ⓑ; Knight— Ⓝ; Pawn— Ⓟ

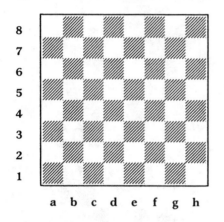

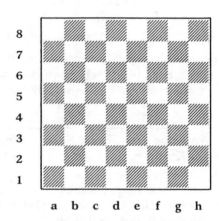

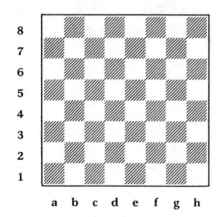

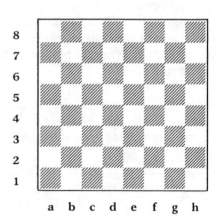

Test Fourteen

1. If you touch one of your pieces which has a legal move, can you move another piece instead?

---

2. Construct a position in which White, with a King, Knight, and pawn, has checkmated a lone Black King.

3. Arrange a Black King, a Black Rook, a Black Bishop, two Black pawns, and a White pawn on a board in such a way that the White pawn can checkmate Black in one move by being promoted into a Knight.

4. Arrange the two Kings and one White pawn on a board in such a way that the White pawn can checkmate Black in one move by being promoted into a Queen or a Rook.

5. Diagram 203—I. White to play and checkmate Black in one move.

---

6. Diagram 203—II. White to play and checkmate Black in one move.

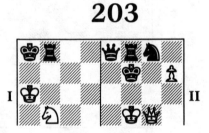

203

I   II

To show different positions on the blank diagrams below, use the following symbols:

WHITE: King— K ; Queen— Q ; Rook— R ; Bishop— B ; Knight— N ; Pawn— P
BLACK: King— Ⓚ; Queen— Ⓠ; Rook— Ⓡ; Bishop— Ⓑ; Knight— Ⓝ; Pawn— Ⓟ

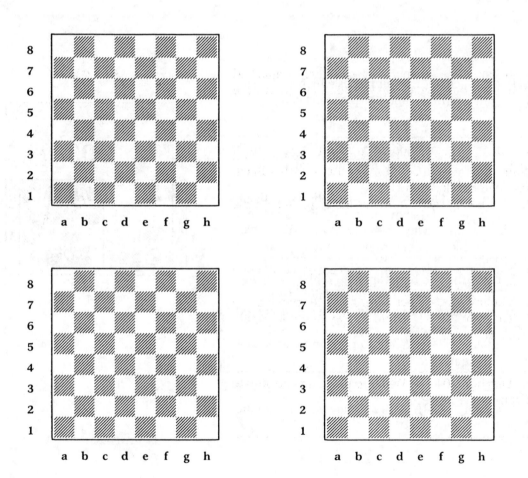

Test Fifteen

1. If you touch an enemy piece which is attacked by one of your own pieces, do you have to capture the enemy piece?

2. Place a Black King, Black Rook, White King, and White Knight on a board in such a way that Black has been checkmated.

3. Can White castle if he has his King on f1 and a Rook on h1?

4. Construct a position in which a pawn can move to any of four squares without itself being under attack at any time, either before or after moving.

5. Diagram 204—I. White to play and checkmate Black in one move.

6. Diagram 204—II. White to play and checkmate Black in one move.

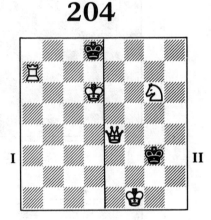

204

I   II

To show different positions on the blank diagrams below, use the following symbols:

WHITE: King— K ; Queen— Q ; Rook— R ; Bishop— B ; Knight— N ; Pawn— P

BLACK: King— Ⓚ ; Queen— Ⓠ ; Rook— Ⓡ ; Bishop— Ⓑ ; Knight— Ⓝ ; Pawn— Ⓟ

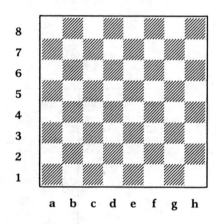

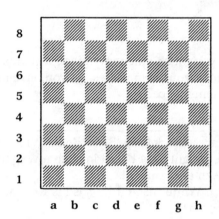

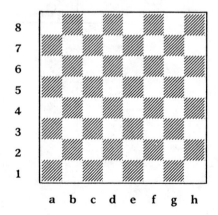

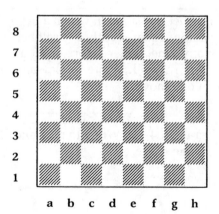

Test Sixteen

1. If a player's King is checked by a Knight or a pawn, can the player get his King out of check by putting one of his men in the way to block the check?

2. Place a Black King, Black Knight, Black pawn, White King, and White pawn on a board in such a way that Black has been checkmated.

3. Can Black castle if he has his King on e8 and a Rook on g8?

4. Set up a position in which each player has only a King and pawn, and Black has been checkmated.

5. Diagram 205—1. White to play and checkmate Black in one move.

6. Diagram 205—II. White to play and checkmate Black in one move.

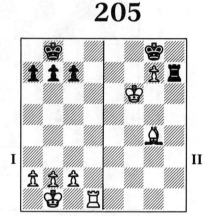

205

I   II

To show different positions on the blank diagrams below, use the following symbols:

WHITE: King— K ; Queen— Q ; Rook— R ; Bishop— B ; Knight— N ; Pawn— P
BLACK: King— (K); Queen— (Q); Rook— (R); Bishop— (B); Knight— (N); Pawn— (P)

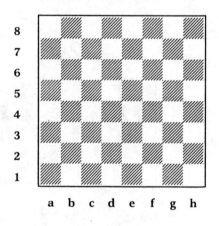

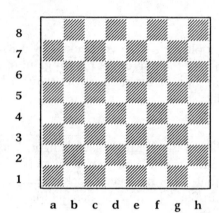

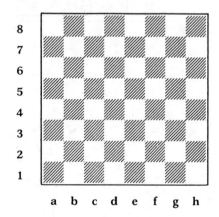

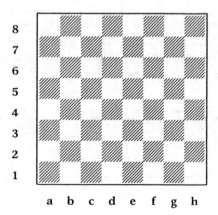

Test Seventeen

1. What is the least number of moves in which a pawn starting from its home square can change into a Queen?

---

2. Construct a position in which White, with a Queen and Bishop, has checkmated a lone Black King.

3. Place a Black King, Black pawn, White King, and White Rook on a board in such a way that White can give perpetual check to the Black King.

4. Place a Black King, a Black Knight, two Black Bishops, and a White Knight on a board in such a way that the White Knight can give perpetual check.

5. Diagram 206—I. White to play and checkmate Black in one move.

---

6. Diagram 206—II. White to play and checkmate Black in one move.

206

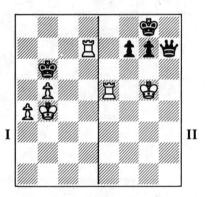

I   II

To show different positions on the blank diagrams below, use the following symbols:

WHITE: King— K ; Queen— Q ; Rook— R ; Bishop— B ; Knight— N ; Pawn— P

BLACK: King— Ⓚ; Queen— Ⓠ; Rook— Ⓡ; Bishop— Ⓑ; Knight— Ⓝ; Pawn— Ⓟ

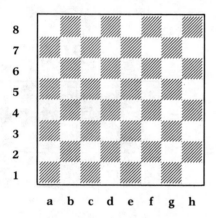

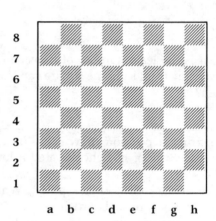

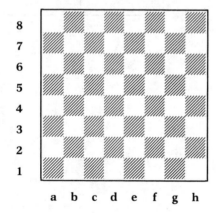

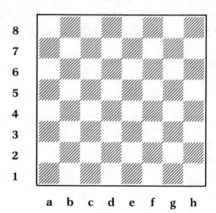

Test Eighteen

1. Is it possible in a game for White to have pawns on g2, h2, and h3 at the same time?

2. Place a Black King, Black Bishop, Black pawn, White King, and White pawn on a board in such a way that Black has been checkmated.

3. Suppose that White has a King and a pawn, and Black has just a King. Make up a position in which White can checkmate Black in one move only by promoting his pawn to a Queen.

4. Suppose that White has a King and a pawn, and Black has just his King. Make up a position in which White would stalemate Black if he promoted his pawn to Queen.

5. Diagram 207—I. White to move and checkmate Black in one move.

6. Diagram 207—II. White to move and checkmate Black in one move.

207

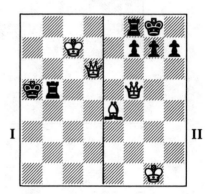

I   II

To show different positions on the blank diagrams below, use the following symbols:

WHITE: King— K ; Queen— Q ; Rook— R ; Bishop— B ; Knight— N ; Pawn— P

BLACK: King— Ⓚ; Queen— Ⓠ; Rook— Ⓡ; Bishop— Ⓑ; Knight— Ⓝ; Pawn— Ⓟ

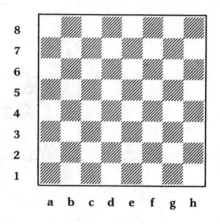

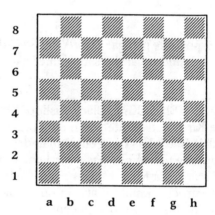

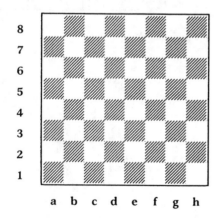

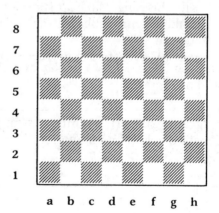

Test Nineteen

1. Can the a-pawn ever get to the e-file? If so, how?

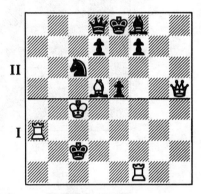

208

2. Construct a position in which White, with a Queen and a Knight, has checkmated a lone Black King.

3. Suppose that White has his King on e1 and a Rook on h1, while Black has a Bishop on e3 and there is no man on f2. Can White castle?

4. Suppose that White has his King on e1 and a Rook on h1, while Black has a Bishop on h3 and there is no man on g2. Can White castle?

5. Diagram 208—I. White to play and checkmate Black in one move.

6. Diagram 208—II. White to play and checkmate Black in one move.

To show different positions on the blank diagrams below, use the following symbols:

WHITE: King— K ; Queen— Q ; Rook— R ; Bishop— B ; Knight— N ; Pawn— P

BLACK: King— (K); Queen— (Q); Rook— (R); Bishop— (B); Knight— (N); Pawn— (P)

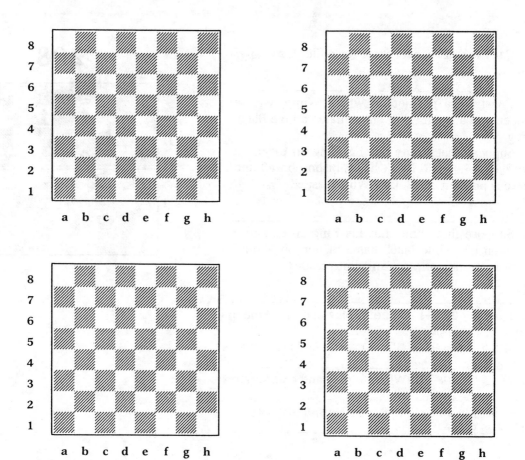

Test Twenty

1. How many moves does a Knight need to get from c3 to e5? Write down its route.

---

2. Construct a position in which four White pawns, without help from their King or other pieces, have checkmated the Black King.

3. Suppose that White has a King and a pawn, and Black has just his King. Make up a position in which the White pawn can become a Queen, but would stalemate Black if it did so, while by becoming a Rook instead, it could checkmate Black the move after it becomes a Rook.

4. Suppose that White has a King and two pawns, and Black has a King and one pawn. Make up a position in which the White pawn is ready to reach the last rank, but would stalemate Black if it turned either into a Queen or a Rook.

5. Diagram 209—I. White to play and checkmate Black in one move.

---

6. Diagram 209—II. White to play and checkmate Black in one move.

209

I   II

To show different positions on the blank diagrams below, use the following symbols:

WHITE: King— K ; Queen— Q ; Rook— R ; Bishop— B ; Knight— N ; Pawn— P
BLACK: King— Ⓚ; Queen— Ⓠ; Rook— Ⓡ; Bishop— Ⓑ; Knight— Ⓝ; Pawn— Ⓟ

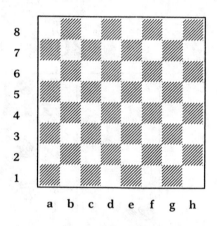

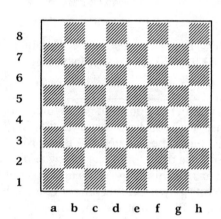

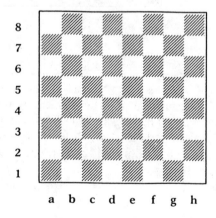

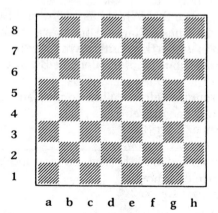

Answers To Test One

1. The a3-f8 diagonal crosses the d-file at d6.
2. Diagram 210.

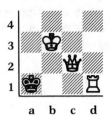

3. Diagram 211.

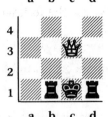

4. Diagram 212.

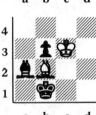

5. Diagram 213.

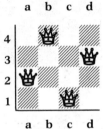

6. There is one Black pawn too many in Diagram 190. After any one of the nine pawns are removed, White can checkmate Black in one move.

If we remove the pawn on
a) a7, then 1. Qb1-b6#
b) b7, then 1. Nd8-c6#
c) c4, then 1. Qb1-b4#
d) d3, then 1. Qb1-e4#
e) e3, then 1. Bg1xf2#
f) f2, then 1. Bg1xe3#
g) f7, then 1. Nd8-e6#
h) g6, then 1. Rg8-g4#
i) h3, then 1. Rh1-h4#

Answers To Test Two

1. The b8-h2 diagonal crosses the 4th rank at f4.
2. Diagram 214.

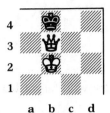

3. Diagram 215.

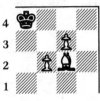

4. Diagram 216. 1. c5xb6#.

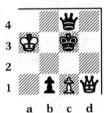

5. Diagram 217.

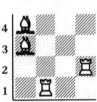

6. Diagram 191. a) The Black King would be checkmated on e3. b) The Black King would be stalemated on h1. c) If we place the Black King on a8, White could checkmate it with one move by Qg4-c8#.

Answers To Test Three

1. The most number of Queens that a player can have is nine (the original Queen plus eight Queens promoted from pawns).

2. Diagram 218.

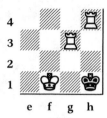

3. Diagram 219.

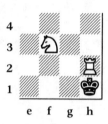

4. Diagram 220.

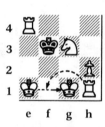

White has made half of his castling move by placing his King on g1. Now he checkmates the Black King by making the other half of the move, i.e. by moving his h1 Rook to f1.

5. Diagram 221.

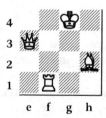

6. **1. Nd3-e5#** checkmates all ten Black Kings in Diagram 192.

Answers To Test Four

1. The most number of Rooks that a player can have is ten (the two original Rooks plus eight Rooks promoted from pawns).

2. Diagram 222.

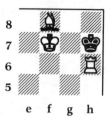

3. Diagram 223.

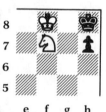

4. Diagram 224.

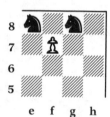

The pawn can turn into any of four different pieces upon reaching the last rank, and since in this case it can reach the last rank in three different ways, it has a total of twelve different possible moves:

   1–4: **1. f7xe8** (Q, R, B, or N)
   2–8: **1. f7-f8** (Q, R, B, or N)
9–12: **1. f7xg8** (Q, R, B, or N)

5. Diagram 225.

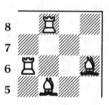

6. The catch in Diagram 193 is that you can't solve the problem without knowing what Black's last move was. It was in fact **... d7-d5.** Now you can see that White can checkmate Black in one move by capturing en passant: **1. e5xd6 e.p.#.**

Answers To Test Five

1. The most number of Bishops that one player can have is ten (the two original ones plus eight Bishops promoted from pawns).

2. Diagram 226.

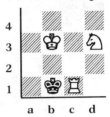

3. Diagram 227.

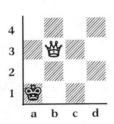

4. Diagram 228.

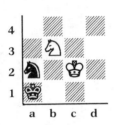

5. Diagram 229.

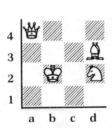

6. Neither Black nor White can avoid checkmating the opponent in Diagram 194. Any move by White checkmates Black, and any move by Black checkmates White!

Answers To Test Six

1. The most number of Knights that one player can have is ten (the two original ones plus eight Knights promoted from pawns).

2. Diagram 230.

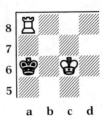

3. Diagram 231.

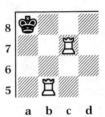

4. Diagram 232.

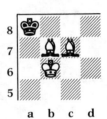

5. Diagram 233.

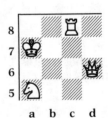

6. White checkmates Black in Diagram 195 by **1. Qc2xh7#.**

Answers To Test Seven

1. A pawn that reaches the last rank cannot remain a pawn, it MUST be promoted to any other piece (except the King) of its own color.

2. Diagram 234.

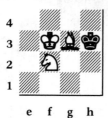

3. Diagram 235.

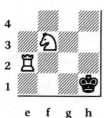

4. Diagram 236.

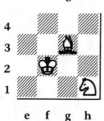

5. Diagram 237.

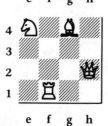

6. White checkmates Black in one move in Diagram 196 by **1. Qf3xf7#**.

Answers To Test Eight

1. No, a pawn cannot ever turn into a King. When a pawn reaches the last rank, it can and must be promoted into any piece of its own color except a King.

2. Diagram 238.

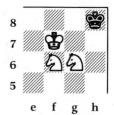

3. Diagram 239.

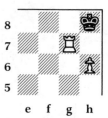

4. Diagram 240.

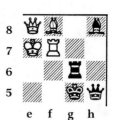

5. Diagram 241.

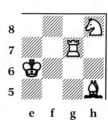

6. White checkmates Black in one move in Diagram 197 by **1. Qf6-g7#**.

Answers To Test Nine

1. Yes, a player can castle when one of his Rooks is attacked, or even when both of them are.

2. Diagram 242.

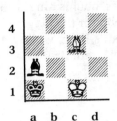

3. Diagram 243.

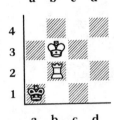

4. Diagram 244.

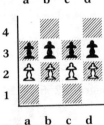

White and Black each have a total of six different pawn moves available.

5. Diagram 245. No.

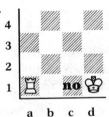

6. White checkmates Black in one move in Diagram 198 by 1. Qc5-f8#.

Answers To Test Ten

1. Yes, castling is permitted if the Rook crosses a square attacked by an enemy man but the King doesn't.

2. Diagram 246.

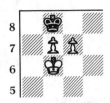

3. Diagram 247. **a)** 1. c7-c8Q#; **b)** 1. c7-c8R#; **c)** 1. c7xd8Q#; **d)** 1. c7xd8R#.

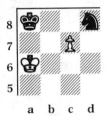

4. Diagram 248.

5. Diagram 249. **1. b7-b8B#.**

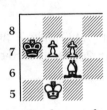

6. White checkmates Black in one move in Diagram 199 by **1. Qg4-d4#.**

Answers To Test Eleven

1. No. En passant capturing is only possible when the opponent's pawn has moved two squares in a single move..

2. Diagram 250.

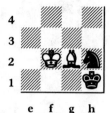

3. Diagram 251.

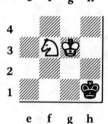

4. Diagram 252.

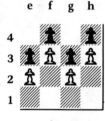

5. Diagram 253. No.

6. White checkmates Black in one move in Diagram 200 by **1. Kc6-c7#.**

Answers To Test Twelve

1. Checkmate is when a King is in check and cannot get out of it. Stalemate is when the player whose turn it is to move has no legal moves, but his King is not in check. Checkmate is a win for the player who checkmates his opponent's King, while stalemate is a draw.

2. Diagram 254.

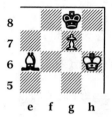

3. Diagram 255.

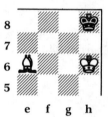

4. Diagram 256.

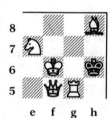

a) 1. Qf5-g6#; **b)** 1. Rg5-h5#; **c)** 1. Bh8-g7#; **d)** 1. Ne7-g8#.

5. Diagram 257.

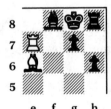

1. ... Kg8-h7; 2. Be6-f5 + Kh7-g8; 3. Bf5-e6 + Kg8-h7 4. Be6-f5 + etc: perpetual check.

6. White checkmates Black in one move in Diagram 201 by **1. f6-f7#.**

Answers To Test Thirteen

1. Only the pawn on f4 can be captured en passant by the Black pawn on e4. The pawn on d4 could only have been captured en passant as soon as White had played d2-d4..

2. Diagram 258.

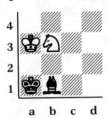

3. Diagram 259.

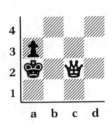

1. ... Ka2-a1 2. Qc2-c1 + Ka1-a2 3. Qc1-c2 + Ka2-a1 4. Qc2-c1 +: perpetual check.

4. Diagram 260.

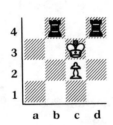

5. In Diagram 202—I, White checkmates by **1. Nd4-c2#.**

6. The catch in Diagram 202—II is that you don't know whether the White King or the Rook on h1 have already moved. Actually, neither one of them has, so that White can castle and checkmate Black: **1. 0-0#.**

Answers To Test Fourteen

1. No. You must move the piece which you touched, if it has a legal move. Don't forget: "Touch — Move"!.

2. Diagram 261.

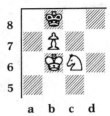

3. Diagram 262. **1. c7-c8N#.**

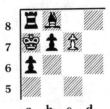

4. Diagram 263. a) **1. d7-d8Q#.** b) **1. d7-d8R#.**

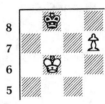

5. In Diagram 203—I, White checkmates by **1. Nb5-c7#.**

6. In Diagram 203—II, White checkmates by **1. h7-h8N#.**

Answers To Test Fifteen

1. If you touch one of your opponent's pieces which is attacked by one of your own pieces, you must capture the piece which you touched.

2. Diagram 264.

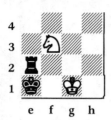

3. Diagram 265. No.

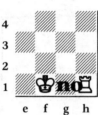

4. Diagram 266. **a) 1. f2xe3; b) 1. f2-f3; c) 1. f2-f4; d) f2xg3.**

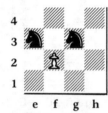

5. In Diagram 204—I, White checkmates by **1. Ra7-a8#.**

6. In Diagram 204—II, White checkmates by **1. Qe4-g2#.**

Answers To Test Sixteen

1. If your King is checked by a pawn or a Knight, the only ways of getting out of check are by moving your King or capturing the checking man..

2. Diagram 267.

3. Diagram 268. No.

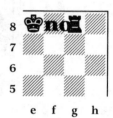

4. Diagram 269.

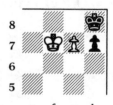

5. In Diagram 205—I, White checkmates by **1. Rd1-d8#.**

6. In Diagram 205—II, White checkmates by **1. Bg4-e6#.**

Answers To Test Seventeen

1. A pawn needs to make at least five moves from its starting position to become a Queen.

2. Diagram 270.

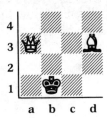

3. Diagram 271.

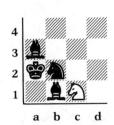

1. ... Ka1-a2 **2.** Rd1-d2 + Ka2-b1 **3.** Rd2-d1 + Kb1-a2 **4.** Rd1-d2 + etc.: perpetual check.

4. Diagram 272.

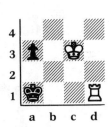

1. ... Ka2-a1 **2.** Nc1-b3 + Ka1-a2 **3.** Nb3-c1 + Ka2-a1 **4.** Nc1-b3 + etc.: perpetual check.

5. In Diagram 206—I, White checkmates by **1. a4-a5#.**

6. In Diagram 206—II, White checkmates by **1. Re5-e8#.**

Answers To Test Eighteen

1. No. A White pawn can get to h3 only by moving up one square from h2 or by capturing from g2. So when the h2 and g2 pawns are still on their home squares, it is impossible for a White pawn to be on h3.

2. Diagram 273.

3. Diagram 274. **1. d7-d8Q#.**

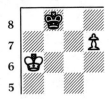

4. Diagram 275. **1. c7-c8Q stalemate.**

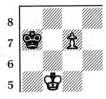

5. In Diagram 207—I, White checkmates by **1. Qd6-a3#.**

6. In Diagram 207—II, White checkmates by **1. Qf5xh7#.**

Answers To Test Nineteen

1. The a-pawn can get to the e-file by capturing four enemy men.

2. Diagram 276.

3. Diagram 277. No.

4. Diagram 278. No.

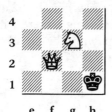

5. In Diagram 208—I, White checkmates by **1. Ra3-a2#.**

6. In Diagram 208—II, White checkmates by **1. Qh5xf7#.**

Answers To Test Twenty

1. A Knight on c3 needs four moves to get to e5. e.g., **Nc3-e4-c5-d3-e5.**

2. Diagram 279.

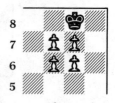

3. Diagram 280. **a) 1. f7-f8Q stalemate; b) 1. f7-f8R Kh7-h6 2. Rf8-h8#.**

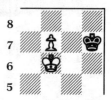

4. Diagram 281. **a) 1. f7-f8Q stalemate; b) 1. f7-f8R stalemate.**

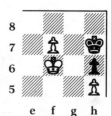

5. In Diagram 209—I, White checkmates by **1. Ba3-c1#.**

6. In Diagram 209—II, White checkmates by **1. Qg5xg7#.**

ROMAN PELTS

Born in Odessa, Ukraine, on August 11, 1937, Roman Pelts holds the rank of FIDE master. But he is best known as one of the most respected chess trainers in the world. Since founding the Roman Pelts Chess Studio, first in Montreal and later in Toronto, he has taught hundreds of students and is commonly regarded as Canada's top chess teacher.

FM Pelts left the former Soviet Union in 1977, taking with him the notes on which *Comprehensive Chess Course* is based. During his years in the Soviet Union, he quickly gained name as a coming young master, finishing second in the Russian Championship for Young Masters. But he soon found teaching chess to be more fulfilling and challenging than playing the game.

In 1959, FM Pelts founded in Odessa a chess school, and among his first pupils were several children, who later became famous grandmasters, including Lev Alburt (the co-author of *Comprehensive Chess Course*), Semyon Palatnik and Vladimir Tukmakov. He was awarded the prestigious title of "Honored Coach." In 1971, he served as coach for the Soviet national student team, which included among its members future FIDE world champion Anatoly Karpov and future title candidate Alexander Beliavsky.

Along with Mark Dvoretsky, FM Pelts is among the most innovative of chess teachers and trainers. He instructs children and adults who are just beginning in chess and top-rated players who need the services of an experienced coach. "One of the most important teaching principles," states FM Pelts, "is to provide students only the knowledge they need at their given level of development. Give them too much, they bog down in detail; give them too little, they do not receive proper training in the basics."

FM Pelts is in demand as a chess teacher and lecturer throughout both Canada and the United States. He is a leading proponent of putting chess into Canada's public schools and has organized numerous tournaments for children. "I firmly believe," he states, "that chess sharpens the minds of kids and contains a value beyond its role of being, quite simply, the world's premier game."

LEV ALBURT

Grandmaster Lev Alburt was born in Orenburg, Russia, on August 21, 1945. For many years, he lived in Odessa, a Ukrainian city located on the Black Sea. A three-time champion of the Ukraine (1972-74), he became European Cup champion in 1976. In 1979, while in West Germany for a chess competition, he defected. Since 1979, GM Alburt has made his home in New York City. In his adopted country, he continues to play chess and "to enjoy the best Russian food anywhere in the United States." He has also returned to his earlier love of teaching chess to those who wish to learn the royal game.

This three-time U.S. Champion (1984, 1985, and 1990), who first taught chess in the former Soviet Union under the direction of many-time world champion Mikhail Botvinnik, nowadays conducts classes at chess camps, teaches and trains some of America's strongest young players under the auspices of the American Chess Foundation, and lectures at clubs throughout the United States. In addition, GM Alburt conducts clinics for scholastic coaches on how better to teach chess to their students. One memorable high point was a speech to the Harvard Russian Research Center on the role of chess in Soviet politics.

As a teacher, GM Alburt is at the forefront of finding new ways to teach chess to students ranging from young children to adults who wish to take up the game. *Comprehensive Chess Course* is one of the products of what is sometimes called "the new chess pedagogy." He frequently works on lessons with IM Mark Dvoretsky, who is commonly regarded as the world's outstanding chess trainer.

Currently GM Alburt often conducts chess lessons by both telephone and mail — having developed course plans for both kinds of instruction. He can be reached by writing to Lev Alburt, P.O. Box 534, Gracie Station, New York, N.Y. 10028.

Other books by GM Alburt include *Test and Improve your Chess*, published by Pergamon Press, and *The Alekhine for the Tournament Player* (co-authored with Eric Schiller), published by Batsford.

"Chess is a game for life," GM Alburt says, " and that means children who learn chess not only improve their ability to reason clearly but also have a pastime that will never fail them as they grow older."

To Order Additional Books:

Contact your local Bookseller or complete the form below

Please send me the following items:

❏ *Comprehensive Chess Course (Volumes I and II come* **in one large book!)**   *$42.00*

❏ *Comprehensive Chess Course Vol. I* (Learn Chess in 12 Lessons)   *$16.95*

❏ *Comprehensive Chess Course Vol. II* (From Beginner to Tournament Player)

                                                                                        $28.95

❏ *Chess Tactics for the Tournament Player*   *$19.95*

❏ *The King in Jeopardy* (The Best Techniques for Attack and Defense)   *$19.95*

Add $4.00 per order for shipping. *All orders will be shipped the same/next day by second-day delivery Priority Mail.*

Send books to:

_____
Name

_____
Street

_____
City   State   Zip Code

To receive an autographed copy, please print name and desired inscription on the following line:

_____

Mail your order and check to:

Lev Alburt
P.O. Box 534 Gracie Station • New York, NY 10028-0005

For credit card orders, call toll-free at (800) 247-6553. Unfortunately, autographs are not available on credit card orders.

Lev Alburt teaches students of all ages and strengths and is available for lessons by telephone, mail or in-person. For further information contact GM Alburt at the above address or phone him at (212) 794-8706.

To Order Additional Books:

Contact your local Bookseller or complete the form below

Please send me the following items:

❏ *Comprehensive Chess Course (Volumes I and II come* **in one large book!)**   ***$42.00***

❏ *Comprehensive Chess Course Vol. I* (Learn Chess in 12 Lessons)   ***$16.95***

❏ *Comprehensive Chess Course Vol. II* (From Beginner to Tournament Player)

     $28.95

❏ *Chess Tactics for the Tournament Player*   ***$19.95***

❏ *The King in Jeopardy* (The Best Techniques for Attack and Defense)   ***$19.95***

Add $4.00 per order for shipping. ***All orders will be shipped the same/next day by second-day delivery Priority Mail.***

Send books to:

_____
Name

_____
Street

_____
City   State   Zip Code

To receive an autographed copy, please print name and desired inscription on the following line:

_____

Mail your order and check to:

Lev Alburt
P.O. Box 534 Gracie Station • New York, NY 10028-0005

For credit card orders, call toll-free at (800) 247-6553. Unfortunately, autographs are not available on credit card orders.

Lev Alburt teaches students of all ages and strengths and is available for lessons by telephone, mail or in-person. For further information contact GM Alburt at the above address or phone him at (212) 794-8706.

To Order Additional Books:

Contact your local Bookseller or complete the form below

Please send me the following items:

❏ *Comprehensive Chess Course (Volumes I and II come* in one large book!)   *$42.00*

❏ *Comprehensive Chess Course Vol. I* (Learn Chess in 12 Lessons)   *$16.95*

❏ *Comprehensive Chess Course Vol. II* (From Beginner to Tournament Player)   *$28.95*

❏ *Chess Tactics for the Tournament Player*   *$19.95*

❏ *The King in Jeopardy* (The Best Techniques for Attack and Defense)   *$19.95*

Add $4.00 per order for shipping. *All orders will be shipped the same/next day by second-day delivery Priority Mail.*

Send books to:

_____
Name

_____
Street

_____
City   State   Zip Code

To receive an autographed copy, please print name and desired inscription on the following line:

_____

Mail your order and check to:

Lev Alburt

P.O. Box 534 Gracie Station • New York, NY 10028-0005

For credit card orders, call toll-free at (800) 247-6553. Unfortunately, autographs are not available on credit card orders.

Lev Alburt teaches students of all ages and strengths and is available for lessons by telephone, mail or in-person. For further information contact GM Alburt at the above address or phone him at (212) 794-8706.